PENGUIN MODERN CLASSICS

PARABLES FOR THE THEATRE

Bertolt Brecht was, and still is, one of the most controversial figures in modern European theatre. He was born in Augsburg, the son of a manufacturer, in 1898, and studied natural science and philosophy in Munich and Berlin. His first play *Baal* was written in 1918, and he wrote thirty-nine others before his death. The best known are *The Threepenny Opera* (1928), *The Life of Galileo* (1939), *Mother Courage and Her Children* (1939), *The Good Woman of Setzuan* (1941) and *The Caucasian Chalk Circle* (1945). A great many of Brecht's plays were, like Shakespeare's, adaptations, but in his hands they became completely fresh works.

When the Nazis came to power, Brecht lived successively in Denmark, Sweden, Finland, and the U.S.A. In 1948 he accepted an offer from the East German government to return to Berlin where, with his wife, he founded the famous Berliner Ensemble in 1949. He died in 1956.

Parables for the Theatre

Two Plays by Bertolt Brecht

The Good Woman of Setzuan
The Caucasian Chalk Circle

Revised English Versions
by Eric Bentley

Penguin Books

Penguin Books Ltd, Harmondsworth, Middlesex, England
Viking Penguin Inc., 40 West 23rd Street, New York, New York 10010, U.S.A.
Penguin Books Australia Ltd, Ringwood, Victoria, Australia
Penguin Books Canada Limited, 2801 John Street, Markham, Ontario, Canada L3R 1B4
Penguin Books (N.Z.) Ltd, 182–190 Wairau Road, Auckland 10, New Zealand

Der gute Mensch von Sezuan first published in Berlin 1953
Copyright © Suhrkamp Verlag, 1955
This translation copyright by Eric Bentley, 1947, as an unpublished MS.
Copyright © Eric Bentley, 1956, 1961
Epilogue copyright © Eric Bentley, 1965

Der Kaukasische Kreidekreis first published at Potsdam 1949
Copyright © Suhrkamp Verlag, 1954
This translation copyright by Eric Bentley, 1947, as an unpublished MS.
Copyright © Eric Bentley, 1961, 1963
Prologue copyright © Eric Bentley, 1959

Parables for the Theatre, Two Plays by Bertolt Brecht
Copyright by Eric Bentley, 1948, as a published book
Introduction copyright © Eric Bentley, 1965

Hard-cover edition published by Oxford University Press, London

Published in Penguin Books 1966
Reprinted 1968, 1970, 1971, 1973, 1975 (twice), 1977, 1979, 1980, 1982, 1983, 1985, 1987

On the back cover, the quotations from *Drama from Ibsen to Brecht*
by Raymond Williams are used by kind permission of Chatto & Windus

Made and printed in Great Britain by
Hazell Watson & Viney Limited,
Member of the BPCC Group,
Aylesbury, Bucks
Set in Monotype Bembo

All rights reserved. These plays may not be acted,
read aloud to an audience, broadcast, televised,
performed or presented in any way, as a whole or
in part, without permission. Inquiries should be addressed
to International Copyright Bureau,
26 Charing Cross Road, London W.C.2

Except in the United States of America,
this book is sold subject to the condition
that it shall not, by way of trade or otherwise,
be lent, re-sold, hired out, or otherwise circulated
without the publisher's prior consent in any form of
binding or cover other than that in which it is
published and without a similar condition
including this condition being imposed
on the subsequent purchaser

Contents

ACKNOWLEDGEMENT. The translator wishes to acknowledge the contribution of Mrs Maja Apelman to the first version of this book, as published in 1948.

Introduction

By Eric Bentley

BERTOLT BRECHT wrote *Der gute Mensch von Sezuan* in Scandinavia at the end of the nineteen-thirties, and *Der kaukasische Kreidekreis* in California in the early and middle forties. The former was originally dedicated to his wife Helene Weigel, to whose playing it was ideally suited. Even the male part of the role would have been nothing new for her: she had played the Young Comrade in *The Measures Taken.* The actress Luise Rainer has stated that *The Caucasian Chalk Circle* was written for her, and that is plausible, since she had played the role equivalent to Grusha's in Klabund's *Circle of Chalk*, without which Brecht's would probably never have been thought of.

Yet, in fact, neither of these distinguished ladies was to 'create' the role seemingly written for her. *The Good Woman* had its world première in Zurich during World War II, when Frau Weigel was a refugee in America. *The Caucasian Chalk Circle* had its world première without benefit of professional actors altogether. (That the latter event took place in Northfield, Minnesota, is not unconnected with the first publication of the present book.)

Late in 1941 Brecht had crossed the U.S.S.R. on the Trans-Siberian Railway and had then sailed across the Pacific to San Pedro, California. I was doing my first year of teaching at the time in the University of California at Los Angeles, and one of my students, who had got himself a hand printing press, wanted to print some poems. Another student said that a German poet was in town and had no translator. The name was Brecht – I was not aware of ever having heard it, though another writer on Brecht has pictured me listening to *Threepenny Opera* records as an Oxford undergraduate in the middle thirties. I arranged to see the poet with a view to translating several of his poems for my student's press.

Herr Brecht was living in a very small frame house in Santa Monica, and I was shown into his bedroom, which was also his study. He had few or no books. But there was a typewriter, and copies of *Freies Deutschland* – which I later found to be a Communist magazine published in Mexico – were strewn about. In the typewriter was the very thin paper, folded double, which I later knew to be characteristic of the man. It was on this paper – the kind used for carbon copies when you have no onion-skin – that I first saw any of the work of Brecht. He handed me a couple of sheets of it while he looked over the samples of my own work I had brought along.

My impression of the man himself is hard to recapture at this distance in time. It is possible that I took Brecht for a truly proletarian writer on the score of his current lack of cash and his general style of living and dress. This would no doubt have been naïve of me. Yet the charm and power of the encounter had their source in just this *naïveté*, and especially in the fact that I had no sense of being in the company of a famous man. Quite a contrast to those meetings with Brecht which young people were to have in the nineteen-fifties, when the cropped head and the tie-less shirt were well known in advance from a score of photographs and a hundred anecdotes! For all I knew, Brecht might have had a trunkful of ties under the bed, and it could have been by chance that he was tie-less at the time . . . or, as I say, it could have been because he was a 'proletarian writer'.

Most famous writers, of course, would have made sure that before I left after our first interview I did have a sense of their fame. Remarkable about Brecht was that he didn't bother about this. Here we see the real human value of what I came later to recognize as a certain deliberate depersonalization of things which Brecht brought about. He did not try to find out much about me. He did not invite me to find out much about him. As in his plays, two people would encounter each other for the sake of what they have to do together. I was a student of German and of poetry. He was a German and had written some poems. *I* would therefore translate some of *him*.

On the spot. And with his collaboration. For he already knew enough English to have a pretty shrewd idea whether a given expression corresponded to the German. 'Freilich, ich lebe in finsteren Zeiten!' That was the first line on one of the bits of tissue paper he had handed me. What did it mean? 'Finstere Zeiten' are 'dark ages'. Was the reference to *the* Dark Ages? (I had no idea of the context.) 'Nein, nein!' said the staccato voice. Then, after a puff at the cigar (not for me 'the famous cigar'): 'Nein, ich meine *diese* Zeiten, Herr Bentley, *unsere* – auch in Los Angeles kann es finster sein, nicht wahr?' He was teasing me a little. That, too, I would later regard as characteristic. At the time it was simply new. . . . Well, what about 'freilich', what did one say in English for that? I suggested many things: 'actually', 'of course', 'oh, yes', 'it's true'. To each one, the quiet yet sharp voice said: 'Nein! Nein!' And Brecht shook his head very decisively. We were discovering together that in our effort to translate his poetry we could not get past the very first word.

The poetry, says Robert Frost, is the untranslatable part. This truth was empirically confirmed by Brecht and myself, but luckily it is a truth which all are agreed in advance to defy, and a half-truth at that. A lot of poetry just as problematical as Brecht's has come down to us in more languages than one – with whatever changes along the way. Although something must have happened to my student's hand press, for I never saw anything in print from it, I had begun translating Bertolt Brecht and am still doing so now, nearly a quarter of a century later.

For a while nothing was said about publication. But then Brecht wanted his poem 'To the German Soldiers in the East' to come out. With him it was always a matter of the place and the time to publish something, considered not personally or 'literarily', but politically: people in America should now read what he had to say about the German armies in Russia. So I translated that poem and sent it to *Partisan Review*. The choice was politically inept, since the editors were violently anti-Communist, but then, being anti-Communist, they knew about Brecht, which at that date other editors didn't. In fact, *Partisan* had run a 'big' article about him in 1941. I was a little upset when Dwight Macdonald, rejecting the poem for the magazine, told me how outrageous he considered its contents to be. (In 1965 an editor of *Partisan* was to ask me please not to fight the Cold War when criticizing the Brecht theatre in East Berlin. Well, it is good that times change.) 'To the German Soldiers in the East' finally appeared in Ray B. West's magazine, the *Rocky Mountain Review*.

Meanwhile, I had my first sizeable assignment from Brecht: to translate, if not for cash on the line, at any rate for possible publication and performance, his full-length play *The Private Life of the Master Race*. This sequence of scenes about life under the Nazis had just been staged in German in New York City by Berthold Viertel, whom I had got to know, and it was Viertel who urged upon Brecht the possibility of an English-language production there, if a translation was on hand. By this time I was teaching at Black Mountain College in North Carolina, and the first performance of the English-language *Private Life* took place in the unlikely environment of the South. My students and I even broadcast a good deal of it on the Asheville radio. And when we did a staged reading of the whole play at the college, the composer Fritz Cohen performed at the organ. I recall a version of the Horst Wessel Song with magnificently distorted harmonies.

The plan to do the play in New York did not die but unfolded too slowly. The war was almost over when finally it was put on, and the public would not wish to hear another word about the Nazis for fifteen or twenty years. Also, the show itself was badly messed up. Brecht must have suspected from the beginning that it would be, for when he asked what the production outfit was called, and was told 'The Theatre of All Nations', he had replied: 'It's too many.'

But Brecht publication in America had begun to get under way. Up to 1940 only the *Threepenny Novel* had been published, and that by a publisher whose interest in Brecht was non-existent. The first publisher to show real interest was Jay Laughlin, founder and owner of New Directions. He had brought out a translation of *Mother Courage* in 1941. He had *Private Life of the Master Race* ready in 1944. Around this time even warmer interest in Brecht was shown by the firm of Reynal and Hitchcock, and Brecht signed a contract with them for an edition of his collected works, of which I was to be general editor. How much happier, as well as simpler, the history of American Brecht publishing would have been had the plan gone through! But Curtice Hitchcock, whose brainchild it was, died soon after; the firm was sold to Harcourt, Brace; and Harcourt did not take over the Brecht project.

It proved impossible to interest any other publisher at that time in taking on the collected works of Brecht. Faced with this new situation, Brecht asked me to get individual plays published whenever opportunity offered and by whatever publishing house. Until 1960 I found only one publisher who would take on a volume of Brecht at all, and I got him published largely by the device of choosing his plays for inclusion in my drama anthologies. Even this sometimes seemed eccentric to publishers. For example, at Doubleday's, when *Threepenny Opera* was included in my *Modern Theatre*, my editor-in-chief, Jason Epstein, who otherwise never objected to any of my choices, inquired: 'What are we doing publishing an opera libretto?'

The one publisher to agree to bring out a volume of Brecht in these lean years was the University of Minnesota Press, which issued *Parables for the Theatre* in 1948. It cannot be said the publication created a sensation, or that the Press expected

it to. But in the fifties Brecht caught on. *Good Woman* and
Chalk Circle were triumphantly produced in many countries,
and Minnesota was able to lease paperback rights on the *Parables* to Grove Press in New York and London. Thereafter this
became the best known of all Brecht books in English-speaking
countries. And the two plays were performed far more than
any of Brecht's others in British and American theatres.

I have mentioned the world première of *The Caucasian
Chalk Circle*. That was at Carleton College, Northfield, Minnesota, in the spring of 1948. The same spring *The Good
Woman* had its American première at Hamline University, St
Paul, Minnesota. All the more enterprising colleges then began
doing the parables, and professional activity followed along at
its lower rate of speed. I accepted an invitation to direct the
first professional production of *The Caucasian Chalk Circle* at
Hedgerow Theatre, near Philadelphia, in the summer of 1948.
Meanwhile Uta Hagen had done a staged reading of *The
Good Woman* in New York; she was later to play the title role
in the first full production of the play in New York. Around
1950 *The Caucasian Chalk Circle* was among the small group
of plays which brought together in Chicago the gifted people
who would later be identified as members of 'Second City'
and 'The Compass'. (I well recall the struggle we had getting
any royalties out of them.) Both the parables eventually became plays that all the more ambitious professional theatres
knew they had to do. The Actor's Workshop of San Francisco
did *The Caucasian Chalk Circle* in 1963; the Minnesota Theatre
Company followed suit in 1965; and in 1966 it had its
New York première at The Lincoln Centre Repertory
Theatre.

A word about the text. It, too, has developed with the years.
What Brecht said he wanted, for his first appearances in print
in the United States, was a faithful word-for-word reproduction of the German. This he got, save for some errors which
were caught later, in the first edition published by Minnesota.

The only significant omission from the book at that time was that of the Prologue to *The Caucasian Chalk Circle*. For the manuscript was delivered to the publishers at about the time of Brecht's appearance before the House Un-American Activities Committee in Washington (October 1947). It was on advice from him that the appearance of this Prologue was postponed. From which incident have come two false rumours: one, that the Prologue was written later and so had not been part of Brecht's original draft of the play; two, that the omission was made on my initiative and so constituted editorial interference. It should be added that when an author says, 'Let's not include such and such a passage till later', he may well not foresee *for how long* he is postponing its inclusion. To insert a prologue, the printer has to redo a whole play. The Prologue to *The Caucasian Chalk Circle*, though found in the German manuscript Brecht sent me in 1946, did not appear in English until the *Tulane Drama Review* printed it at my request in 1959. Soon thereafter, it turned up in the Grove Evergreen paperback edition of the play.

Perhaps all good foreign plays should be published first in a very literal translation and subsequently in various attempts at a true equivalent, even, if necessary, in 'adaptations'. Some plays can have high literary quality in another language and at the same time be fairly literal transcriptions. Others have not proved so amenable. (I put it thus cautiously to allow for the possibility that some or all of them might prove so amenable at some future time.) Brecht toyed with the idea of his plays always being literally translated for publication and freely adapted for performance. But even this is not a perfect formula. Whenever the stage version is more plausible, has more character, more charm, vivacity, edge, or whatnot, reasonable readers will prefer it not only in the theatre but in the study: for it is more readable. Hence, when I had to discard the literal translation of *The Good Woman* for stage purposes, the non-literal text that resulted was adjudged preferable by publishers and readers as well as producers and spectators. For the Phoenix Theatre production (New York, 1956) I decided to ignore the literal translation altogether and, working again with the German, to make a completely new rendering for the stage. Since all the larger libraries have copies of the first Minnesota edition, anyone who is curious about this can look up for himself what the differences are. The 1956 text does amount to 'adaptation' in the sense that some passages have not been translated at all but deliberately omitted or changed. Luckily, the author was still alive when these changes were proposed, and when I last saw Brecht (June 1956) he approved them in principle. (He was not interested in inspecting the script line by line and probably was not well enough to do so in any case.)

In English, things have to be said more tersely than in German. Hence, English translations from German should always come out shorter than the original. Sometimes that is a matter of phraseology only: each sentence should come out shorter. But at other times the very thought and substance of a German text has to be made more compact in English, and in this case whole sentences of the original have to go. Now once you start this more drastic kind of 'cutting' you also find yourself obliged to bridge the 'gaps' you have made with new writing. This is one of the ways in which translation becomes adaptation. . . . It did so in the reworking of *The Good Woman*, and those who wish to know exactly what Brecht said in every detail will, as I say, have to go to the German or the first Minnesota edition. Reprinted here is the stage version used at the Phoenix, plus only the Epilogue which was not used in that show. (Since Grove Press ran precisely the Phoenix text without the Epilogue, yet another false rumour circulated, and was exploited to compound the misunderstanding created by the rumour about the omitted Prologue to *Chalk Circle*: Brecht was *for the second time* being touched up by a translator hostile to Marxism. The coupling of the two rumours did not, of course, make sense, since the printings that omitted the Epilogue to *Good Woman* contained the Prologue to *Chalk Circle*. Anyhow, the present volume contains both.)

For stage purposes, I found that everything in *The Good Woman* had to be said more briefly and swiftly in English than in the German, and I think the reader too will appreciate a terser, lighter-textured piece of reading matter. I would not make this identical statement about *The Caucasian Chalk Circle*. It is not an easier play to turn into English, but it is far less abstract and more poetic. Consequently, the obligation to keep each phrase is far greater, and the result of keeping each – or nearly each – phrase seems a gain, rather than a loss. This does not mean that as soon as one has written out an 'accurate' translation one has finished work. There remains an endless labour, this time not of trimming, cutting, and reshaping scenes, but of weighing one word against another, one phrase against another, and, finally, of trying to achieve a style that might serve as *the* style of this play. The renewed work on *The Good Woman*, since the method meant going back to zero, seemed more radical and while it lasted was indeed more intensive, yet in the end even more work may have been put in on *Chalk Circle*, though this work was done a little at a time and was wholly a matter of details. (A work of art is an accumulation of details.) Many of the changes made in the English text of *Chalk Circle* were incorporated in the Grove Evergreen printings of the early sixties. Many others are first printed in the present edition. Of special use to me in the selection of new readings was the Harvard University production of the play (1960) directed by John Hancock.

One has always to ask of a Brecht translation what German text it is based on, since Brecht himself was forever changing what he wrote. The present English versions are in principle based on manuscripts supplied by Brecht in 1945.* This fact

---

* In the spring of 1946 Reynal and Hitchcock brought out my book *The Playwright as Thinker* in which Brecht's as yet unpublished 'parables' were summarized.

explains one or two things that might otherwise appear anom-
alous. For example, 'Sezuan' was a city in the manuscript,
though later it would be identified as 'Szechwan', which is a
province. Since Brecht obviously could not have had in mind
a province when he wrote 'a city', I consider the original reading sounder and have kept it. It is in line with all Brecht's other
'misunderstandings' of geography and even with a stage tradi-
tion that goes back to things like the 'seacoast of Bohemia' in
Shakespeare. *Der kaukasische Kreidekreis* was published in sub-
stantially the form I knew it, not in the book editions, but in
the 1949 Brecht Supplement of the magazine *Sinn und Form*.
Since nothing in the English of *Chalk Circle* is in the nature of
'free adaptation', the reader can be sure that if he finds any passage there that is not in the German text he consults it *is* taken
from some other German text. For instance, the scabrous bit
about the soldier getting an erection from stabbing was omitted from later German versions. Conversely, at Brecht's request, I inserted some rhymes to introduce the Azdak trial
scenes which had not been found in the 1945 manuscript. To
sum up: the present rendering of *Chalk Circle* claims to provide a line-by-line equivalent of the German, though 'the
German' is itself a flexible term in this context; while the present
Good Woman adheres far less closely to *Der gute Mensch von
Sezuan*, which, however, readers can find translated literally
in the first Minnesota edition.

Berlin
March 1965
New York
March 1966

The Good Woman of Setzuan

CHARACTERS

WONG, *a water seller*
THREE GODS
SHEN TE, *a prostitute, later a shopkeeper*
MRS SHIN, *former owner of Shen Te's shop*
A FAMILY OF EIGHT (*husband, wife, brother, sister-in-law,
  grandfather, nephew, niece, boy*)
AN UNEMPLOYED MAN
A CARPENTER
MRS MI TZU, *Shen Te's landlady*
YANG SUN, *an unemployed pilot, later a factory manager*
AN OLD WHORE
A POLICEMAN
AN OLD MAN
AN OLD WOMAN, *his wife*
MR SHU FU, *a barber*
MRS YANG, *mother of Yang Sun*
MR CHENG
PRIEST
WAITER
WORKERS
GENTLEMEN, VOICES, CHILDREN (*three*), *etc.*

Prologue

At the gates of the half-Westernized city of Setzuan. Evening.
WONG *the water seller introduces himself to the audience.*

WONG: I sell water here in the city of Setzuan. It isn't easy.
When water is scarce, I have long distances to go in search
of it, and when it is plentiful, I have no income. But in our
part of the world there is nothing unusual about poverty.
Many people think only the gods can save the situation. And
I hear from a cattle merchant – who travels a lot – that some
of the highest gods are on their way here at this very moment. Informed sources have it that heaven is quite disturbed
at all the complaining. I've been coming out here to the city
gates for three days now to bid these gods welcome. I want
to be the first to greet them. What about those fellows over
there? No, no, they *work*. And that one there has ink on his
fingers, he's no god, he must be a clerk from the cement
factory. *Those* two are another story. They look as though
they'd like to beat you. But gods don't need to beat you, do
they? [THREE GODS *appear.*] What about those three? Old-
fashioned clothes – dust on their feet – they *must* be gods!
[*He throws himself at their feet.*] Do with me what you will,
illustrious ones!

FIRST GOD [*with an ear trumpet*]: Ah! [*He is pleased.*] So we
were expected?

WONG [*giving them water*]: Oh, yes. And I *knew* you'd come.

FIRST GOD: We need somewhere to stay the night. You know
of a place?

WONG: The whole town is at your service, illustrious ones!
What sort of a place would you like?

[*The* GODS *eye each other.*]

FIRST GOD: Just try the first house you come to, my son.

WONG: That would be Mr Fo's place.

FIRST GOD: Mr Fo.

WONG: One moment! [*He knocks at the first house.*]

VOICE FROM MR FO'S: No!

　　　[WONG *returns a little nervously.*]

WONG: It's too bad. Mr Fo isn't in. And his servants don't dare do a thing without his consent. He'll have a fit when he finds out who they turned away, won't he?

FIRST GOD [*smiling*]: He will, won't he?

WONG: One moment! The next house is Mr Cheng's. Won't he be thrilled!

FIRST GOD: Mr Cheng.

　　　[WONG *knocks.*]

VOICE FROM MR CHENG'S: Keep your gods. We have our own troubles!

WONG [*back with the* GODS]: Mr Cheng is very sorry, but he has a houseful of relations. I think some of them are a bad lot, and naturally, he wouldn't like you to see them.

THIRD GOD: Are we so terrible?

WONG: Well, only with bad people, of course. Everyone knows the province of Kwan is always having floods.

SECOND GOD: Really? How's that?

WONG: Why, because they're so irreligious.

SECOND GOD: Rubbish. It's because they neglected the dam.

FIRST GOD [*to* SECOND]: Sh! [*To* WONG] You're still in hopes, aren't you, my son?

WONG: Certainly. All Setzuan is competing for the honour! What happened up to now is pure coincidence. I'll be back. [*He walks away, but then stands undecided.*]

SECOND GOD: What did I tell you?

THIRD GOD: It *could* be pure coincidence.

SECOND GOD: The same coincidence in Shun, Kwan, and Setzuan? People just aren't religious any more, let's face the fact. Our mission has failed!

FIRST GOD: Oh come, we might run into a good person any minute.

THIRD GOD: How did the resolution read? [*Unrolling a scroll and reading from it*] 'The world can stay as it is if enough people are found [*at the word 'found' he unrolls it a little more*] living lives worthy of human beings.' Good people, that is. Well, what about this water seller himself? *He's* good, or I'm very much mistaken.

SECOND GOD: You're very much mistaken. When he gave us a drink, I had the impression there was something odd about the cup. Well, look! [*He shows the cup to the* FIRST GOD.]

FIRST GOD: A false bottom!

SECOND GOD: The man is a swindler.

FIRST GOD: Very well, count *him* out. That's one man among millions. And as a matter of fact, we only need one on *our* side. These atheists are saying, 'The world must be changed because no one can *be* good and *stay* good.' No one, eh? I say: let us find one – just one – and we have those fellows where we want them!

THIRD GOD [*to* WONG]: Water seller, is it so hard to find a place to stay?

WONG: Nothing could be easier. It's just me. I don't go about it right.

THIRD GOD: Really? [*He returns to the others.*]
   [*A* GENTLEMAN *passes by.*]

WONG: Oh dear, they're catching on. [*He accosts the* GENTLE-MAN.] Excuse the intrusion, dear sir, but three gods have just turned up. Three of the very highest. They need a place for the night. Seize this rare opportunity – to have real gods as your guests!

GENTLEMAN [*laughing*]: A new way of finding free rooms for a gang of crooks. [*Exit* GENTLEMAN.]

WONG [*shouting at him*]: Godless rascal! Have you no religion, gentlemen of Setzuan? [*Pause.*] Patience, illustrious ones!

[*Pause.*] There's only one person left. Shen Te, the prostitute. She *can't* say no. [*Calls up to a window*] Shen Te!

    [SHEN TE *opens the shutters and looks out.*]

WONG: Shen Te, it's Wong. *They're* here, and nobody wants them. Will you take them?

SHEN TE: Oh, no, Wong, I'm expecting a gentleman.

WONG: Can't you forget about him for tonight?

SHEN TE: The rent has to be paid by tomorrow or I'll be out on the street.

WONG: This is no time for calculation, Shen Te.

SHEN TE: Stomachs rumble even on the Emperor's birthday, Wong.

WONG: Setzuan is one big dung hill!

SHEN TE: Oh, very well! I'll hide till my gentleman has come and gone. Then I'll take them. [*She disappears.*]

WONG: They mustn't see her gentleman or they'll know what she is.

FIRST GOD [*who hasn't heard any of this*]: I think it's hopeless. [*They approach* WONG.]

WONG [*jumping, as he finds them behind him*]: A room has been found, illustrious ones! [*He wipes sweat off his brow.*]

SECOND GOD: Oh, good.

THIRD GOD: Let's see it.

WONG [*nervously*]: Just a minute. It has to be tidied up a bit.

THIRD GOD: Then we'll sit down here and wait.

WONG [*still more nervous*]: No, no! [*Holding himself back*] Too much traffic, you know.

THIRD GOD [*with a smile*]: Of course, if you *want* us to move. [*They retire a little. They sit on a doorstep.*]

    [WONG *sits on the ground.*]

WONG [*after a deep breath*]: You'll be staying with a single girl – the finest human being in Setzuan!

THIRD GOD: That's nice.

WONG [*to the audience*]: They gave me such a look when I picked up my cup just now.

THIRD GOD: You're worn out, Wong.

WONG: A little, maybe.

FIRST GOD: Do people here have a hard time of it?

WONG: The good ones do.

FIRST GOD: What about yourself?

WONG: You mean I'm not good. That's true. And I don't have an easy time either!

[During this dialogue, a GENTLEMAN has turned up in front of Shen Te's house, and has whistled several times. Each time WONG has given a start.]

THIRD GOD [to WONG, softly]: Psst! I think he's gone now.

WONG [confused and surprised]: Ye-e-es.

[The GENTLEMAN has left now, and SHEN TE has come down to the street.]

SHEN TE [softly]: Wong! [Getting no answer, she goes off down the street.]

[WONG arrives just too late, forgetting his carrying pole.]

WONG [softly]: Shen Te! Shen Te! [To himself] So she's gone off to earn the rent. Oh dear, I can't go to the gods again with no room to offer them. Having failed in the service of the gods, I shall run to my den in the sewer pipe down by the river and hide from their sight! [He rushes off.]

[SHEN TE returns, looking for him, but finding the GODS. She stops in confusion.]

SHEN TE: You are the illustrious ones? My name is Shen Te. It would please me very much if my simple room could be of use to you.

THIRD GOD: Where is the water seller, Miss . . . Shen Te?

SHEN TE: I missed him, somehow.

FIRST GOD: Oh, he probably thought you weren't coming, and was afraid of telling us.

THIRD GOD [picking up the carrying pole]: We'll leave this with you. He'll be needing it.

[Led by SHEN TE, they go into the house. It grows dark, then light. Dawn. Again escorted by SHEN TE, who leads them *through the half-light with a little lamp, the* GODS *take their leave.*]

FIRST GOD: Thank you, thank you, dear Shen Te, for your elegant hospitality! We shall not forget! And give our thanks to the water seller – he showed us a good human being.

SHEN TE: Oh, *I'm* not good. Let me tell you something: when Wong asked me to put you up, I hesitated.

FIRST GOD: It's all right to hesitate if you then go ahead! And in giving us that room you did much more than you knew. You proved that good people still exist, a point that has been disputed of late – even in heaven. Farewell!

SECOND GOD: Farewell!

THIRD GOD: Farewell!

SHEN TE: Stop, illustrious ones! I'm not sure you're right. I'd like to be good, it's true, but there's the rent to pay. And that's not all: I sell myself for a living. Even so I can't make ends meet, there's too much competition. I'd like to honour my father and mother and speak nothing but the truth and not covet my neighbour's house. I should love to stay with one man. But how? How is it done? Even breaking a few of your commandments, I can hardly manage.

FIRST GOD [*clearing his throat*]: These thoughts are but, um, the misgivings of an unusually good woman!

THIRD GOD: Good-bye, Shen Te! Give our regards to the water seller!

SECOND GOD: And above all: be good! Farewell!

FIRST GOD: Farewell!

THIRD GOD: Farewell! [*They start to wave good-bye.*]

SHEN TE: But everything is so expensive, I don't feel sure I can do it!

SECOND GOD: That's not in our sphere. We never meddle with economics.

THIRD GOD: One moment. [*They stop.*] Isn't it true she might do better if she had more money?

SECOND GOD: Come, come! How could we ever account for it Up Above?

FIRST GOD: Oh, there are ways. [*They put their heads together and confer in dumb show. To* SHEN TE, *with embarrassment*] As you say you can't pay your rent, well, um, we're not paupers, so of course we *insist* on paying for our room. [*Awkwardly thrusting money into her hands*] There! [*Quickly*] But don't tell anyone! The incident is open to misinterpretation.

SECOND GOD: It certainly is!

FIRST GOD [*defensively*]: But there's no law against it! It was never decreed that a god mustn't pay hotel bills!

　[*The* GODS *leave.*]

I

A small tobacco shop. The shop is not as yet completely furnished and hasn't started doing business.

SHEN TE [*to the audience*]: It's three days now since the gods left. When they said they wanted to pay for the room, I looked down at my hand, and there was more than a thousand silver dollars! I bought a tobacco shop with the money, and moved in yesterday. I don't own the building, of course, but I can pay the rent, and I hope to do a lot of good here. Beginning with Mrs Shin, who's just coming across the square with her pot. She had the shop before me, and yesterday she dropped in to ask for rice for her children. [*Enter* MRS SHIN. *Both women bow.*] How do you do, Mrs Shin.

MRS SHIN: How do you do, Miss Shen Te. You like your new home?

SHEN TE: Indeed, yes. Did your children have a good night?

MRS SHIN: In that hovel? The youngest is coughing already.

SHEN TE: Oh, dear!

MRS SHIN: You're going to learn a thing or two in these slums.

SHEN TE: Slums? That's not what you said when you sold me the shop!

MRS SHIN: Now don't start nagging! Robbing me and my innocent children of their home and then calling it a slum! That's the limit! [*She weeps.*]

SHEN TE [*tactfully*]: I'll get your rice.

MRS SHIN: And a little cash while you're at it.

SHEN TE: I'm afraid I haven't sold anything yet.

MRS SHIN [*screeching*]: I've got to have it. Strip the clothes from my back and then cut my throat, will you? I know what I'll do: I'll dump my children on your doorstep! [*She snatches the pot out of* SHEN TE'S *hands.*]

SHEN TE: Please don't be angry. You'll spill the rice.

[*Enter an elderly* HUSBAND *and* WIFE *with their shabbily dressed* NEPHEW.]

WIFE: Shen Te, dear! You've come into money, they tell me. And we haven't a roof over our heads! A tobacco shop. We had one too. But it's gone. Could we spend the night here, do you think?

NEPHEW [*appraising the shop*]: Not bad!

WIFE: He's our nephew. We're inseparable!

MRS SHIN: And who are these . . . ladies and gentlemen?

SHEN TE: They put me up when I first came in from the country. [*To the audience*] Of course, when my small purse was empty, they put me out on the street, and they may be afraid I'll do the same to them. [*To the newcomers, kindly*] Come in, and welcome, though I've only one little room for you – it's behind the shop.

HUSBAND: That'll do. Don't worry.

WIFE [*bringing* SHEN TE *some tea*]: We'll stay over here, so we won't be in your way. Did you make it a tobacco shop in memory of your first real home? We can certainly give you a hint or two! That's one reason we came.

MRS SHIN [*to* SHEN TE]: Very nice! As long as you have a few customers too!

HUSBAND: Sh! A customer!

[*Enter an* UNEMPLOYED MAN, *in rags.*]

UNEMPLOYED MAN: Excuse me. I'm unemployed.

[MRS SHIN *laughs.*]

SHEN TE: Can I help you?

UNEMPLOYED MAN: Have you any damaged cigarettes? I thought there might be some damage when you're unpacking.

WIFE: What nerve, begging for tobacco! [*Rhetorically*] Why don't they ask for bread?

UNEMPLOYED MAN: Bread is expensive. One cigarette butt and I'll be a new man.

SHEN TE [*giving him cigarettes*]: That's very important – to be a new man. You'll be my first customer and bring me luck.
[*The* UNEMPLOYED MAN *quickly lights a cigarette, inhales, and goes off, coughing.*]

WIFE: Was that right, Shen Te, dear?

MRS SHIN: If this is the opening of a shop, you can hold the closing at the end of the week.

HUSBAND: I bet he had money on him.

SHEN TE: Oh, no, he said he hadn't!

NEPHEW: How d'you know he wasn't lying?

SHEN TE [*angrily*]: How do you know he was?

WIFE [*wagging her head*]: You're too good, Shen Te, dear. If you're going to keep this shop, you'll have to learn to say no.

HUSBAND: Tell them the place isn't yours to dispose of. Belongs to . . . some relative who insists on all accounts being strictly in order . . .

MRS SHIN: That's right! What do you think you are – a philanthropist?

SHEN TE [*laughingly*]: Very well, suppose I ask you for my rice back, Mrs Shin?

WIFE [*combatively, at* MRS SHIN]: So that's *her* rice?
[*Enter the* CARPENTER, *a small man.*]

MRS SHIN [*who, at the sight of him, starts to hurry away*]: See you tomorrow, Miss Shen Te! [*Exit* MRS SHIN.]

CARPENTER: Mrs Shin, it's you I want!

WIFE [*to* SHEN TE]: Has she some claim on you?

SHEN TE: She's hungry. That's a claim.

CARPENTER: Are you the new tenant? And filling up the shelves already? Well, they're not yours till they're paid for, ma'am. I'm the carpenter, so I should know.

SHEN TE: I took the shop 'furnishings included'.

CARPENTER: You're in league with that Mrs Shin, of course. All right. I demand my hundred silver dollars.

SHEN TE: I'm afraid I haven't got a hundred silver dollars.

CARPENTER: Then you'll find it. Or I'll have you arrested.

WIFE [*whispering to* SHEN TE]: That relative: make it a cousin.

SHEN TE: Can't it wait till next month?

CARPENTER: No!

SHEN TE: Be a little patient, Mr Carpenter, I can't settle all claims at once.

CARPENTER: Who's patient with me? [*He grabs a shelf from the wall.*] Pay up – or I take the shelves back!

WIFE: Shen Te! Dear! Why don't you let your ... cousin settle this affair? [*To* CARPENTER] Put your claim in writing. Shen Te's cousin will see you get paid.

CARPENTER [*derisively*]: Cousin, eh?

HUSBAND: Cousin, yes.

CARPENTER: I know these cousins!

NEPHEW: Don't be silly. He's a personal friend of mine.

HUSBAND: What a man! Sharp as a razor!

CARPENTER: All right. I'll put my claim in writing. [*Puts shelf on floor, sits on it, writes out bill.*]

WIFE [*to* SHEN TE]: He'd tear the dress off your back to get his shelves. Never recognize a claim! That's my motto.

SHEN TE: He's done a job, and wants something in return. It's shameful that I can't give it to him. What will the gods say?

HUSBAND: You did your bit when you took *us* in.

[*Enter the* BROTHER, *limping, and the* SISTER-IN-LAW, *pregnant.*]

BROTHER [*to* HUSBAND *and* WIFE]: So this is where you're hiding out! There's family feeling for you! Leaving us on the corner!

WIFE [*embarrassed, to* SHEN TE]: It's my brother and his wife. [*To them*] Now stop grumbling, and sit quietly in that corner. [*To* SHEN TE] It can't be helped. She's in her fifth month.

SHEN TE: Oh yes. Welcome!

WIFE [*to the couple*]: Say thank you. [*They mutter something.*]

The cups are there. [*To* SHEN TE] Lucky you bought this shop when you did!

SHEN TE [*laughing and bringing tea*]: Lucky indeed!

[*Enter* MRS MI TZU, *the landlady*.]

MRS MI TZU: Miss Shen Te? I am Mrs Mi Tzu, your landlady. I hope our relationship will be a happy one. I like to think I give my tenants modern, personalized service. Here is your lease. [*To the others, as* SHEN TE *reads the lease*] There's nothing like the opening of a little shop, is there? A moment of true beauty! [*She is looking around.*] Not very much on the shelves, of course. But everything in the gods' good time! Where are your references, Miss Shen Te?

SHEN TE: Do I *have* to have references?

MRS MI TZU: After all, I haven't a notion who you are!

HUSBAND: Oh, *we'd* be glad to vouch for Miss Shen Te! We'd go through fire for her!

MRS MI TZU: And who may *you* be?

HUSBAND [*stammering*]: Ma Fu, tobacco dealer.

MRS MI TZU: Where is your shop, Mr ... Ma Fu?

HUSBAND: Well, um, I haven't got a shop – I've just sold it.

MRS MI TZU: I see. [*To* SHEN TE] Is there no one else that knows you?

WIFE [*whispering to* SHEN TE]: Your cousin! Your cousin!

MRS MI TZU: This is a respectable house, Miss Shen Te. I never sign a lease without certain assurances.

SHEN TE [*slowly, her eyes downcast*]: I have ... a cousin.

MRS MI TZU: On the square? Let's go over and see him. What does he do?

SHEN TE [*as before*]: He lives ... in another city.

WIFE [*prompting*]: Didn't you say he was in Shung?

SHEN TE: That's right. Shung.

HUSBAND [*prompting*]: I had his name on the tip of my tongue. Mr ...

SHEN TE [*with an effort*]: Mr ... Shui ... Ta.

HUSBAND: That's it! Tall, skinny fellow!

SHEN TE: Shui Ta!

NEPHEW [*to* CARPENTER]: *You* were in touch with him, weren't you? About the shelves?

CARPENTER [*surlily*]: Give him this bill. [*He hands it over.*] I'll be back in the morning. [*Exit* CARPENTER.]

NEPHEW [*calling after him, but with his eyes on* MRS MI TZU]: Don't worry! Mr Shui Ta pays on the nail!

MRS MI TZU [*looking closely at* SHEN TE]: I'll be happy to make his acquaintance, Miss Shen Te. [*Exit* MRS MI TZU.] [*Pause.*]

WIFE: By tomorrow morning she'll know more about you than you do yourself.

SISTER-IN-LAW [*to* NEPHEW]: This thing isn't built to last. [*Enter* GRANDFATHER.]

WIFE: It's Grandfather! [*To* SHEN TE] Such a good old soul! [*The* BOY *enters.*]

BOY [*over his shoulder*]: Here they are!

WIFE: And the boy, how he's grown! But he always could eat enough for ten. [*Enter the* NIECE.]

WIFE [*to* SHEN TE]: Our little niece from the country. There are more of us now than in your time. The less we had, the more there were of us; the more there were of us, the less we had. Give me the key. We must protect ourselves from unwanted guests. [*She takes the key and locks the door*]. Just make yourself at home. I'll light the little lamp.

NEPHEW [*a big joke*]: I hope her cousin doesn't drop in to-night! The strict Mr Shui Ta! [SISTER-IN-LAW *laughs.*]

BROTHER [*reaching for a cigarette*]: One cigarette more or less . . .

HUSBAND: One cigarette more or less. [*They pile into the cig-arettes. The* BROTHER *hands a jug of wine round.*]

NEPHEW: Mr Shui Ta'll pay for it!

GRANDFATHER [*gravely, to* SHEN TE]: How do you do?

[SHEN TE, *a little taken aback by the belatedness of the greeting, bows. She has the carpenter's bill in one hand, the landlady's lease in the other.*]

WIFE: How about a bit of a song? To keep Shen Te's spirits up?

NEPHEW: Good idea. Grandfather: you start!

SONG OF THE SMOKE

GRANDFATHER:
    I used to think (before old age beset me)
      That brains could fill the pantry of the poor.
    But where did all my cerebration get me?
      I'm just as hungry as I was before.
        So what's the use?
          See the smoke float free
      Into ever colder coldness!
        It's the same with me.

HUSBAND:
    The straight and narrow path leads to disaster
      And so the crooked path I tried to tread.
    That got me to disaster even faster.
      (They say we shall be happy when we're dead.)
        So what's the use?
          See the smoke float free
      Into ever colder coldness!
        It's the same with me.

NIECE:
    You older people, full of expectation,
      At any moment now you'll walk the plank!
    The future's for the younger generation!
      Yes, even if that future is a blank.
        So what's the use?
          See the smoke float free
      Into ever colder coldness!
        It's the same with me.

NEPHEW [*to the* BROTHER]: Where'd you get that wine?

SISTER-IN-LAW [*answering for the* BROTHER]: He pawned the sack of tobacco.

HUSBAND [*stepping in*]: What? That tobacco was all we had to fall back on! You pig!

BROTHER: *You'd* call a man a pig because your wife was frigid! Did you refuse to drink it? [*They fight. The shelves fall over.*]

SHEN TE [*imploringly*]: Oh don't! Don't break everything! Take it, take it all, but don't destroy a gift from the gods!

WIFE [*disparagingly*]: This shop isn't big enough. I should never have mentioned it to Uncle and the others. When *they* arrive, it's going to be disgustingly overcrowded.

SISTER-IN-LAW: And did you hear our gracious hostess? She cools off quick!

[*Voices outside. Knocking at the door.*]

UNCLE'S VOICE: Open the door!

WIFE: Uncle? Is that you, Uncle?

UNCLE'S VOICE: Certainly, it's me. Auntie says to tell you she'll have the children here in ten minutes.

WIFE [*to* SHEN TE]: I'll have to let him in.

SHEN TE [*who scarcely hears her*]:

> The little lifeboat is swiftly sent down
> Too many men too greedily
> Hold on to it as they drown.

Ia

Wong's den in a sewer pipe.

WONG [*crouching there*]: All quiet! It's four days now since I left the city. The gods passed this way on the second day. I heard their steps on the bridge over there. They must be a long way off by this time, so I'm safe. [*Breathing a sigh of relief, he curls up and goes to sleep. In his dream the pipe becomes transparent, and the* GODS *appear. Raising an arm, as if in self-defence*] I know, I know, illustrious ones! I found no one to give you a room – not in all Setzuan! There, it's out. Please continue on your way!

FIRST GOD [*mildly*]: But you did find someone. Someone who took us in for the night, watched over us in our sleep, and in the early morning lighted us down to the street with a lamp.

WONG: It was . . . Shen Te that took you in?

THIRD GOD: Who else?

WONG: And I ran away! 'She isn't coming,' I thought, 'she just can't afford it.'

GODS [*singing*]:

O you feeble, well-intentioned, and yet feeble chap
Where there's need the fellow thinks there is no goodness!
When there's danger he thinks courage starts to ebb away!
Some people only see the seamy side!
What hasty judgement! What premature desperation!

WONG: I'm *very* ashamed, illustrious ones.

FIRST GOD: Do us a favour, water seller. Go back to Setzuan. Find Shen Te, and give us a report on her. We hear that she's come into a little money. Show interest in her goodness – for no one can be good for long if goodness is not in demand. Meanwhile we shall continue the search, and find other good people. After which, the idle chatter about the impossibility of goodness will stop!

[*The* GODS *vanish.*]

2

A knocking.

WIFE: Shen Te! Someone at the door. Where is she anyway?

NEPHEW: She must be getting the breakfast. Mr Shui Ta will pay for it.

[*The* WIFE *laughs and shuffles to the door. Enter* MR SHUI TA *and the* CARPENTER.]

WIFE: Who is it?

SHUI TA: I am Miss Shen Te's cousin.

WIFE: What??

SHUI TA: My name is Shui Ta.

WIFE: Her cousin?

NEPHEW: Her cousin?

NIECE: But that was a joke. She hasn't got a cousin.

HUSBAND: So early in the morning?

BROTHER: What's all the noise?

SISTER-IN-LAW: This fellow says he's her cousin.

BROTHER: Tell him to prove it.

NEPHEW: Right. If you're Shen Te's cousin, prove it by getting the breakfast.

SHUI TA [*whose régime begins as he puts out the lamp to save oil; loudly, to all present, asleep or awake*]: Would you all please get dressed! Customers will be coming! I wish to open my shop!

HUSBAND: *Your* shop? Doesn't it belong to our good friend Shen Te?

[SHUI TA *shakes his head.*]

SISTER-IN-LAW: So we've been cheated. Where *is* the little liar?

SHUI TA: Miss Shen Te has been delayed. She wishes me to tell you there will be nothing she can do – now I am here.

WIFE [*bowled over*]: I thought she was good!

NEPHEW: Do you have to believe *him*?

HUSBAND: I don't.

NEPHEW: Then do something.

HUSBAND: Certainly! I'll send out a search party at once. You, you, you, and you, go out and look for Shen Te. [*As the* GRANDFATHER *rises and makes for the door*] Not you, Grandfather, you and I will hold the fort.

SHUI TA: You won't find Miss Shen Te. She has suspended

her hospitable activity for an unlimited period. There are too many of you. She asked me to say: this is a tobacco shop, not a gold mine.

HUSBAND: Shen Te never said a thing like that. Boy, food! There's a bakery on the corner. Stuff your shirt full when they're not looking!

SISTER-IN-LAW: Don't overlook the raspberry tarts.

HUSBAND: And don't let the policeman see you.

[*The* BOY *leaves.*]

SHUI TA: Don't you depend on this shop now? Then why give it a bad name by stealing from the bakery?

NEPHEW: Don't listen to him. Let's find Shen Te. She'll give him a piece of her mind.

SISTER-IN-LAW: Don't forget to leave us some breakfast.

[BROTHER, SISTER-IN-LAW, *and* NEPHEW *leave.*]

SHUI TA [*to the* CARPENTER]: You see, Mr Carpenter, nothing has changed since the poet, eleven hundred years ago, penned these lines:

A governor was asked what was needed
To save the freezing people in the city.
He replied:
'A blanket ten thousand feet long
To cover the city and all its suburbs.'

[*He starts to tidy up the shop.*]

CARPENTER: Your cousin owes me money. I've got witnesses. For the shelves.

SHUI TA: Yes, I have your bill. [*He takes it out of his pocket.*] Isn't a hundred silver dollars rather a lot?

CARPENTER: No deductions! I have a wife and children.

SHUI TA: How many children?

CARPENTER: Three.

SHUI TA: I'll make you an offer. Twenty silver dollars.

[*The* HUSBAND *laughs.*]

CARPENTER: You're crazy. Those shelves are real walnut.

SHUI TA: Very well. Take them away.

CARPENTER: What?

SHUI TA: They cost too much. Please take them away.

WIFE: Not bad! [*And she, too, is laughing.*]

CARPENTER [*a little bewildered*]: Call Shen Te, someone! [*To* SHUI TA] She's *good!*

SHUI TA: Certainly. She's ruined.

CARPENTER [*provoked into taking some of the shelves*]: All right, you can keep your tobacco on the floor.

SHUI TA [*to the* HUSBAND]: Help him with the shelves.

HUSBAND [*grins and carries one shelf over to the door where the* CARPENTER *now is*]: Good-bye, shelves!

CARPENTER [*to the* HUSBAND]: You dog! You want my family to starve?

SHUI TA: I repeat my offer. I have no desire to keep my tobacco on the floor. Twenty silver dollars.

CARPENTER [*with desperate aggressiveness*]: One hundred!
    [SHUI TA *shows indifference, looks through the window. The* HUSBAND *picks up several shelves.*]

CARPENTER [*to* HUSBAND]: You needn't smash them against the doorpost, you idiot! [*To* SHUI TA] These shelves were made to measure. They're no use anywhere else!

SHUI TA: Precisely.
    [*The* WIFE *squeals with pleasure.*]

CARPENTER [*giving up, sullenly*]: Take the shelves. Pay what you want to pay.

SHUI TA [*smoothly*]: Twenty silver dollars. [*He places two large coins on the table.*]
    [*The* CARPENTER *picks them up.*]

HUSBAND [*brings the shelves back in*]: And quite enough too!

CARPENTER [*slinking off*]: Quite enough to get drunk on.

HUSBAND [*happily*]: Well, we got rid of *him!*

WIFE [*weeping with fun, gives a rendition of the dialogue just spoken*]: 'Real walnut,' says he. 'Very well, take them away,' says his lordship. 'I have three children,' says he. 'Twenty silver dollars,' says his lordship. 'They're no use anywhere else,' says he. 'Pre-cisely,' said his lordship! [*She dissolves into shrieks of merriment.*]

SHUI TA: And now: go!

HUSBAND: What's that?

SHUI TA: You're thieves, parasites. I'm giving you this chance. Go!

HUSBAND [*summoning all his ancestral dignity*]. That sort deserves no answer. Besides, one should never shout on an empty stomach.

WIFE: Where's that boy?

SHUI TA: Exactly. The boy. I want no stolen goods in this shop. [*Very loudly*] I strongly advise you to leave! [*But they remain seated, noses in the air. Quietly*] As you wish. [SHUI TA *goes to the door. A* POLICEMAN *appears.* SHUI TA *bows.*] I am addressing the officer in charge of this precinct?

POLICEMAN: That's right, Mr, um, what was the name, sir?

SHUI TA: Mr Shui Ta.

POLICEMAN: Yes, of course, sir.

[*They exchange a smile.*]

SHUI TA: Nice weather we're having.

POLICEMAN: A little on the warm side, sir.

SHUI TA: Oh, a little on the warm side.

HUSBAND [*whispering to the* WIFE]: If he keeps it up till the boy's back, we're done for. [*Tries to signal* SHUI TA.]

SHUI TA [*ignoring the signal*]: Weather, of course, is one thing indoors, another out on the dusty street!

POLICEMAN: Oh, quite another, sir!

WIFE [*to the* HUSBAND]: It's all right as long as he's standing in the doorway – the boy will see him.

SHUI TA: Step inside for a moment! It's quite cool indoors. My cousin and I have just opened the place. And we attach the greatest importance to being on good terms with the, um, authorities.

POLICEMAN [*entering*]: Thank you, Mr Shui Ta. It *is* cool!

HUSBAND [*whispering to the* WIFE]: And now the boy *won't* see him.

SHUI TA [*showing* HUSBAND *and* WIFE *to the* POLICEMAN]: Visitors, I think my cousin knows them. They were just leaving.

HUSBAND [*defeated*]: Ye-e-es, we were . . . just leaving.

SHUI TA: I'll tell my cousin you couldn't wait.

[*Noise from the street. Shouts of* 'Stop, Thief!']

POLICEMAN: What's that?

[*The* BOY *is in the doorway with cakes and buns and rolls spilling out of his shirt. The* WIFE *signals desperately to him to leave. He gets the idea.*]

POLICEMAN: No, you don't! [*He grabs the* BOY *by the collar.*] Where's all this from?

BOY [*vaguely pointing*]: Down the street.

POLICEMAN [*grimly*]: So that's it. [*Prepares to arrest the* BOY.]

WIFE [*stepping in*]: And *we* knew nothing about it. [*To the* BOY] Nasty little thief!

POLICEMAN [*dryly*]: Can you clarify the situation, Mr Shui Ta?

[SHUI TA *is silent.*]

POLICEMAN [*who understands silence*]: Aha. You're all coming with me – to the station.

SHUI TA: I can hardly say how sorry I am that *my* establishment . . .

WIFE: Oh, he saw the boy leave not ten minutes ago!

SHUI TA: And to conceal the theft asked a policeman in?

POLICEMAN: Don't listen to her, Mr Shui Ta, I'll be happy to relieve you of their presence one and all! [*To all three*] Out! [*He drives them before him.*]

GRANDFATHER [*leaving last, gravely*]: Good morning!

POLICEMAN: Good morning!

[SHUI TA, *left alone, continues to tidy up.* MRS MI TZU *breezes in.*]

MRS MI TZU: *You're* her cousin, are you? Then have the goodness to explain what all this means – police dragging people from a respectable house! By what right does your Miss Shen Te turn my property into a house of assignation? – Well, as you see, I know all!

SHUI TA: Yes. My cousin has the worst possible reputation: that of being poor.

MRS MI TZU: No sentimental rubbish, Mr Shui Ta. Your cousin was a common . . .

SHUI TA: Pauper. Let's use the uglier word.

MRS MI TZU: I'm speaking of her conduct, not her earnings. But there must have *been* earnings, or how did she buy all this? Several elderly gentlemen took care of it, I suppose. I repeat: this is a respectable house! I have tenants who prefer not to live under the same roof with such a person.

SHUI TA [*quietly*]: How much do you want?

MRS MI TZU [*he is ahead of her now*]: I beg your pardon.

SHUI TA: To reassure yourself. To reassure your tenants. How much will it cost?

MRS MI TZU: You're a cool customer.

SHUI TA [*picking up the lease*]: The rent is high. [*He reads on.*] I assume it's payable by the month?

MRS MI TZU: Not in her case.

SHUI TA [*looking up*]: What?

MRS MI TZU: Six months' rent payable in advance. Two hundred silver dollars.

SHUI TA: Six . . . ! Sheer usury! And where am I to find it?

MRS MI TZU: You should have thought of that before.

SHUI TA: Have you no heart, Mrs Mi Tzu? It's true Shen Te acted foolishly, being kind to all those people, but she'll improve with time. I'll see to it she does. She'll work her fingers to the bone to pay her rent, and all the time be as quiet as a mouse, as humble as a fly.

MRS MI TZU: Her social background . . .

SHUI TA: Out of the depths! She came out of the depths! And before she'll go back there, she'll work, sacrifice, shrink

from nothing. . . . Such a tenant is worth her weight in gold,
Mrs Mi Tzu.

MRS MI TZU: It's silver we were talking about, Mr Shui Ta.
Two hundred silver dollars or . . .

[*Enter the* POLICEMAN.]

POLICEMAN: Am I intruding, Mr Shui Ta?

MRS MI TZU: This tobacco shop is well known to the police,
I see.

POLICEMAN: Mr Shui Ta has done us a service, Mrs Mi Tzu.
I am here to present our official felicitations!

MRS MI TZU: That means less than nothing to me, sir. Mr Shui
Ta, all I can say is: I hope your cousin will find my terms
acceptable. Good day, gentlemen. [*Exit.*]

SHUI TA: Good day, ma'am.

[*Pause.*]

POLICEMAN: Mrs Mi Tzu a bit of a stumbling block, sir?

SKUI TA: She wants six months' rent in advance.

POLICEMAN: And you haven't got it, eh? [SHUI TA *is silent.*]
But surely you can get it, sir? A man like you?

SHUI TA: What about a woman like Shen Te?

POLICEMAN: You're not staying, sir?

SHUI TA: No, and I won't be back. Do you smoke?

POLICEMAN [*taking two cigars, and placing them both in his
pocket*]: Thank you, sir – I see your point. Miss Shen Te – let's
mince no words – Miss Shen Te lived by selling herself.
'What else could she have done?' you ask. 'How else was
she to pay the rent?' True. But the fact remains, Mr Shui Ta,
it is not respectable. Why not? A very deep question. But,
in the first place, love – love isn't bought and sold like cigars,
Mr Shui Ta. In the second place, it isn't respectable to go
waltzing off with someone that's paying his way, so to speak
– it must be for love! Thirdly and lastly, as the proverb has it:
not for a handful of rice but for love! [*Pause. He is thinking
hard.*] 'Well,' you may say, 'and what good is all this wisdom if the milk's already spilt?' Miss Shen Te is what she is.

Is *where* she is. We have to face the fact that if she doesn't get hold of six months' rent pronto, she'll be back on the streets. The question then as I see it – everything in this world is a matter of opinion – the question as I see it is: *how* is she to get hold of this rent? How? Mr Shui Ta: I don't know. [*Pause.*] I take that back, sir. It's just come to me. A husband. We must find her a husband!

[*Enter a little* OLD WOMAN.]

OLD WOMAN: A good cheap cigar for my husband, we'll have been married forty years tomorrow and we're having a little celebration.

SHUI TA: Forty years? And you still want to celebrate?

OLD WOMAN: As much as we can afford to. We have the carpet shop across the square. We'll be good neighbours, I hope?

SHUI TA: I hope so too.

POLICEMAN [*who keeps making discoveries*]: Mr Shui Ta, you know what we need? We need capital. And how do we acquire capital? We get married.

SHUI TA [*to* OLD WOMAN]: I'm afraid I've been pestering this gentleman with my personal worries.

POLICEMAN [*lyrically*]: We can't pay six months' rent, so what do we do? We marry money.

SHUI TA: That might not be easy.

POLICEMAN: Oh, I don't know. She's a good match. Has a nice, growing business. [*To the* OLD WOMAN] What do you think?

OLD WOMAN [*undecided*]: Well –

POLICEMAN: Should she put an ad. in the paper?

OLD WOMAN [*not eager to commit herself*]: Well, if *she* agrees –

POLICEMAN: I'll write it for her. *You* lend us a hand, and *we* write an ad. for you! [*He chuckles away to himself, takes out his notebook, wets the stump of a pencil between his lips, and writes away.*]

SHUI TA [*slowly*]: Not a bad idea.

POLICEMAN: 'What ... *respectable* ... man ... with small capital ... widower ... not excluded ... desires ... marriage ... into flourishing ... tobacco shop?' And now let's add: 'Am ... pretty ...' No! ... 'Prepossessing appearance.'

SHUI TA: If you don't think that's an exaggeration?

OLD WOMAN: Oh, not a bit. I've seen her.

[*The* POLICEMAN *tears the page out of his notebook, and hands it over to* SHUI TA.]

SHUI TA [*with horror in his voice*]: How much luck we need to keep our heads above water! How many ideas! How many friends! [*To the* POLICEMAN] Thank you, sir, I think I see my way clear.

3

Evening in the municipal park. Noise of a plane overhead. YANG SUN, *a young man in rags, is following the plane with his eyes: one can tell that the machine is describing a curve above the park.* YANG SUN *then takes a rope out of his pocket, looking anxiously about him as he does so. He moves toward a large willow. Enter* TWO PROSTITUTES, *one old, the other the* NIECE *whom we have already met.*

NIECE: Hello. Coming with me?

YANG SUN [*taken aback*]: If you'd like to buy me a dinner.

OLD WHORE: Buy you a dinner! [*To the* NIECE] Oh, we know him – it's the unemployed pilot. Waste no time on him!

NIECE: But he's the only man left in the park. And it's going to rain.

OLD WHORE: Oh, how do you know?

[*And they pass by.* YANG SUN *again looks about him, again takes his rope, and this time throws it round a branch of the willow tree. Again he is interrupted. It is the* TWO PROSTITUTES *returning – and in such a hurry they don't notice him.*]

NIECE: It's going to pour!

[*Enter* SHEN TE.]

OLD WHORE: There's that *gorgon* Shen Te! That *drove* your family out into the cold!

NIECE: It wasn't her. It was that cousin of hers. She offered to pay for the cakes. I've nothing against her.

OLD WHORE: I have, though. [*So that* SHEN TE *can hear*] Now where could the little lady be off to? She may be rich now but that won't stop her snatching our young men, will it?

SHEN TE: I'm going to the tea-room by the pond.

NIECE: Is it true what they say? You're marrying a widower – with three children?

SHEN TE: Yes. I'm just going to see him.

YANG SUN [*his patience at breaking point*]: Move on there! This is a park, not a whore-house!

OLD WHORE: Shut your mouth!

[*But the* TWO PROSTITUTES *leave.*]

YANG SUN: Even in the farthest corner of the park, even when it's raining, you can't get rid of them! [*He spits.*]

SHEN TE [*overhearing this*]: And what right have you to scold them? [*But at this point she sees the rope.*] Oh!

YANG SUN: Well, what are you staring at?

SHEN TE: That rope. What is it for?

YANG SUN: Think! Think! I haven't a penny. Even if I had, I wouldn't spend it on you. I'd buy a drink of water. [*The rain starts.*]

SHEN TE [*still looking at the rope*]: What is the rope for? You mustn't!

YANG SUN: What's it to you? Clear out!

SHEN TE [*irrelevantly*]: It's raining.

YANG SUN: Well, don't try to come under this tree.

SHEN TE: Oh, no. [*She stays in the rain.*]

YANG SUN: Now go away. [*Pause.*] For one thing, I don't like your looks, you're bow-legged.

SHEN TE [*indignantly*]: That's not true!

YANG SUN: Well, don't show 'em to me. Look, it's raining. You better come under this tree.

[*Slowly, she takes shelter under the tree.*]

SHEN TE: Why did you want to do it?

YANG SUN: You really want to know? [*Pause.*] To get rid of you! [*Pause.*] You know what a flyer is?

SHEN TE: Oh yes, I've met a lot of pilots. At the tea-room.

YANG SUN: You call *them* flyers? Think they know what a machine is? Just 'cause they have leather helmets? They gave the airfield director a bribe, that's the way *those* fellows got up in the air! Try one of them out sometime. 'Go up to two thousand feet,' tell him, 'then let it fall, then pick it up again with a flick of the wrist at the last moment.' Know what he'll say to that? 'It's not in my contract.' Then again, there's the landing problem. It's like landing on your own backside. It's no different, planes are human. Those fools don't understand. [*Pause.*] And I'm the biggest fool for reading the book on flying in the Peking school and skipping the page where it says: 'We've got enough flyers and we don't need you.' I'm a mail pilot with no mail. You understand that?

SHEN TE [*shyly*]: Yes. I do.

YANG SUN: No, you don't. You'd never understand that.

SHEN TE: When we were little we had a crane with a broken wing. He made friends with us and was very good-natured about our jokes. He would strut along behind us and call out to stop us going too fast for him. But every spring and autumn when the cranes flew over the villages in great swarms, he got quite restless. [*Pause.*] I understand that. [*She bursts out crying.*]

YANG SUN: Don't!

SHEN TE [*quieting down*]: No.

YANG SUN: It's bad for the complexion.

SHEN TE [*sniffing*]: I've stopped. [*She dries her tears on her big sleeve. Leaning against the tree, but not looking at her, he reaches for her face.*]

YANG SUN: You can't even wipe your own face. [*He is wiping it for her with his handkerchief. Pause.*]

SHEN TE [*still sobbing*]: I don't know *anything*!

YANG SUN: You interrupted me! What for?

SHEN TE: It's such a rainy day. You only wanted to do ... *that* because it's such a rainy day. [*To the audience*]

    In our country
    The evenings should never be sombre
    High bridges over rivers
    The grey hour between night and morning
    And the long, long winter:
    Such things are dangerous
    For, with all the misery,
    A very little is enough
    And men throw away an unbearable life.

    [*Pause.*]

YANG SUN: Talk about yourself for a change.

SHEN TE: What about me? I have a shop.

YANG SUN [*incredulous*]: You have a shop, have you? Never thought of walking the streets?

SHEN TE: I did walk the streets. Now I have a shop.

YANG SUN [*ironically*]: A gift of the gods, I suppose!

SHEN TE: How did you know?

YANG SUN [*even more ironical*]: One fine evening the gods turned up saying: here's some money!

SHEN TE [*quickly*]: One fine morning.

YANG SUN [*fed up*]: This isn't much of an entertainment.

    [*Pause.*]

SHEN TE: I can play the zither a little. [*Pause.*] And I can mimic men. [*Pause.*] I got the shop, so the first thing I did was to give my zither away. I can be as stupid as a fish now, I said to myself, and it won't matter.

> I'm rich now, I said
> I walk alone, I sleep alone
> For a whole year, I said
> I'll have nothing to do with a man.

YANG SUN: And now you're marrying one! The one at the tea-room by the pond?

[SHEN TE *is silent.*]

YANG SUN: What do you know about love?

SHEN TE: Everything.

YANG SUN: Nothing. [*Pause.*] Or d'you just mean you enjoyed it?

SHEN TE: No.

YANG SUN [*again without turning to look at her, he strokes her cheek with his hand*]: You like that?

SHEN TE: Yes.

YANG SUN [*breaking off*]: You're easily satisfied, I must say. [*Pause.*] What a town!

SHEN TE: You have no friends?

YANG SUN [*defensively*]: Yes, I have! [*Change of tone.*] But they don't want to hear I'm still unemployed. 'What?' they ask. 'Is there still water in the sea?' You have friends?

SHEN TE [*hesitating*]: Just a . . . cousin.

YANG SUN: Watch him carefully.

SHEN TE: He only came once. Then he went away. He won't be back. [YANG SUN *is looking away.*] But to be without hope, they say, is to be without goodness!

[*Pause.*]

YANG SUN: Go on talking. A voice is a voice.

SHEN TE: Once, when I was a little girl, I fell, with a load of brushwood. An old man picked me up. He gave me a penny too. Isn't it funny how people who don't have very much like to give some of it away? They must like to show what they can do, and how could they show it better than by being kind? Being wicked is just like being clumsy. When we sing a song, or build a machine, or plant some rice, we're being kind. You're kind.

YANG SUN: You make it sound easy.

SHEN TE: Oh, no. [*Little pause.*] Oh! A drop of rain!

YANG SUN: Where'd you feel it?

SHEN TE: Between the eyes.

YANG SUN: Near the right eye? Or the left?

SHEN TE: Near the left eye.

YANG SUN: Oh, good. [*He is getting sleepy.*] So you're through with men, eh?

SHEN TE [*with a smile*]: But I'm not bow-legged.

YANG SUN: Perhaps not.

SHEN TE: Definitely not.

[*Pause.*]

YANG SUN [*leaning wearily against the willow*]: I haven't had a drop to drink all day, I haven't eaten anything for *two* days. I couldn't love you if I tried.

[*Pause.*]

SHEN TE: I like it in the rain.

[*Enter* WONG *the water seller, singing.*]

THE SONG OF THE WATER SELLER IN THE RAIN

'Buy my water,' I am yelling
And my fury restraining
For no water I'm selling
'Cause it's raining, 'cause it's raining!
I keep yelling: 'Buy my water!'
But no one's buying
Athirst and dying
And drinking and paying!
Buy water!
Buy water, you dogs!

Nice to dream of lovely weather!
Think of all the consternation
Were there no precipitation
Half a dozen years together!
   Can't you hear them shrieking: 'Water!'
   Pretending they adore me?
   They all would go down on their knees before me!
   Down on your knees!
   Go down on your knees, you dogs!

What are lawns and hedges thinking?
What are fields and forests saying?
'At the cloud's breast we are drinking!
And we've no idea who's paying!'
   I keep yelling: 'Buy my water!'
   But no one's buying
   Athirst and dying
   And drinking and paying!
   Buy water!
   Buy water, you dogs!

[*The rain has stopped now.* SHEN TE *sees* WONG *and runs toward him.*]

SHEN TE: Wong! You're back! Your carrying pole's at the shop.

WONG: Oh, thank you, Shen Te. And how is life treating *you*?

SHEN TE: I've just met a brave and clever man. And I want to buy him a cup of your water.

WONG [*bitterly*]: Throw back your head and open your mouth and you'll have all the water you need –

SHEN TE [*tenderly*]:
   I want *your* water, Wong
   The water that has tired you so
   The water that you carried all this way
   The water that is hard to sell because it's been raining.
I need it for the young man over there – he's a flyer!

A flyer is a bold man:
Braving the storms
In company with the clouds
He crosses the heavens
And brings to friends in faraway lands
The friendly mail!

[*She pays* WONG, *and runs over to* YANG SUN *with the cup. But* YANG SUN *is fast asleep.*]

SHEN TE [*calling to* WONG, *with a laugh*]: He's fallen asleep! Despair and rain and I have worn him out!

3a

Wong's den. The sewer pipe is transparent, and the GODS *again appear to* WONG *in a dream.*

WONG [*radiant*]: I've seen her, illustrious ones! And she hasn't changed!

FIRST GOD: That's good to hear.

WONG: She loves someone.

FIRST GOD: Let's hope the experience gives her the strength to stay good!

WONG: It does. She's doing good deeds all the time.

FIRST GOD: Ah? What sort? What sort of good deeds, Wong?

WONG: Well, she has a kind word for everybody.

FIRST GOD [*eagerly*]: And then?

WONG: Hardly anyone leaves her shop without tobacco in his pocket – even if he can't pay for it.

FIRST GOD: Not bad at all. Next?

WONG: She's putting up a family of eight.

FIRST GOD [*gleefully,* to the SECOND GOD]: Eight! [*To* WONG] And that's not all, of course!

WONG: She bought a cup of water from me even though it was raining.

FIRST GOD: Yes, yes, yes, all these smaller good deeds!

WONG: Even they run into money. A little tobacco shop doesn't make so much.

FIRST GOD [*sententiously*]: A prudent gardener works miracles on the smallest plot.

WONG: She hands out rice every morning. That eats up half her earnings.

FIRST GOD [*a little disappointed*]: Well, as a beginning ...

WONG: They call her the Angel of the Slums – whatever the carpenter may say!

FIRST GOD: What's this? A carpenter speaks ill of her?

WONG: Oh, he only says her shelves weren't paid for in full.

SECOND GOD [*who has a bad cold and can't pronounce his n's and m's*]: What's this? Not paying a carpenter? Why was that?

WONG: I suppose she didn't have the money.

SECOND GOD [*severely*]: One pays what one owes, that's in our book of rules! First the letter of the law, then the spirit.

WONG: But it wasn't Shen Te, illustrious ones, it was her cousin. She called *him* in to help.

SECOND GOD: Then her cousin must never darken her threshold again!

WONG: Very well, illustrious ones! But in fairness to Shen Te, let me say that her cousin is a businessman.

FIRST GOD: Perhaps we should inquire what is customary? I find business quite unintelligible. But everybody's doing it. Business! Did the Seven Good Kings do business? Did Kung the Just sell fish?

SECOND GOD: In any case, such a thing must not occur again! [*The* GODS *start to leave.*]

THIRD GOD: Forgive us for taking this tone with you, Wong, we haven't been getting enough sleep. The rich recommend us to the poor, and the poor tell us they haven't enough room.

SECOND GOD: Feeble, feeble, the best of them!

FIRST GOD: No great deeds! No heroic daring!

THIRD GOD: On such a *small* scale!

SECOND GOD: Sincere, yes, but what is actually *achieved*?
[*One can no longer hear them.*]

WONG [*calling after them*]: I've thought of something, illustrious ones: Perhaps you shouldn't ask – too – much – all – at – once!

4

The square in front of Shen Te's tobacco shop. Besides Shen Te's place, two other shops are seen: the carpet shop and a barber's. Morning. Outside Shen Te's the GRANDFATHER, *the* SISTER-IN-LAW, *the* UNEMPLOYED MAN, *and* MRS SHIN *stand waiting.*

SISTER-IN-LAW: She's been out all night again.

MRS SHIN: No sooner did we get rid of that crazy cousin of hers than Shen Te herself starts carrying on! Maybe she does give us an ounce of rice now and then, but can you depend on her? Can you depend on her?
[*Loud voices from the barber's.*]

VOICE OF SHU FU: What are you doing in my shop? Get out – at once!

VOICE OF WONG: But sir. They all let me sell . . . [WONG *comes staggering out of the barber's shop pursued by* MR SHU FU, *the barber, a fat man carrying a heavy curling iron.*]

SHU FU: Get out, I said! Pestering my customers with your slimy old water! Get out! Take your cup! [*He holds out the cup.* WONG *reaches out for it.* MR SHU FU *strikes his hand with the curling iron, which is hot.* WONG *howls.*]

SHU FU: You had it coming, my man! [*Puffing, he returns to his shop.*]
[*The* UNEMPLOYED MAN *picks up the cup and gives it to* WONG.]

UNEMPLOYED MAN: You can report that to the police.

WONG: My hand! It's smashed up!

UNEMPLOYED MAN: Any bones broken?

WONG: I can't move my fingers.

UNEMPLOYED MAN: Sit down. I'll put some water on it.

[WONG *sits.*]

MRS SHIN: The water won't cost you anything.

SISTER-IN-LAW: You might have got a bandage from Miss Shen Te till she took to staying out all night. It's a scandal.

MRS SHIN [*despondently*]: If you ask me, she's forgotten we ever existed!

[*Enter* SHEN TE *down the street, with a dish of rice.*]

SHEN TE [*to the audience*]: How wonderful to see Setzuan in the early morning! I always used to stay in bed with my dirty blanket over my head afraid to wake up. This morning I saw the newspapers being delivered by little boys, the streets being washed by strong men, and fresh vegetables coming in from the country on ox carts. It's a long walk from where Yang Sun lives, but I feel lighter at every step. They say you walk on air when you're in love, but it's even better walking on the rough earth, on the hard cement. In the early morning, the old city looks like a great heap of rubbish! Nice, though, with all its little lights. And the sky, so pink, so transparent, before the dust comes and muddies it! What a lot you miss if you never see your city rising from its slumbers like an honest old craftsman pumping his lungs full of air and reaching for his tools, as the poet says! [*Cheerfully, to her waiting guests*] Good morning, everyone, here's your rice! [*Distributing the rice, she comes upon* WONG]. Good morning, Wong, I'm quite light-headed today. On my way over, I looked at myself in all the shop windows. I'd love to be beautiful. [*She slips into the carpet shop.*]

[MR SHU FU *has just emerged from his shop.*]

SHU FU [*to the audience*]: It surprises me how beautiful Miss Shen Te is looking today! I never gave her a passing thought before. But now I've been gazing upon her comely form for exactly three minutes! I begin to suspect I am in love with her. She is overpoweringly attractive! [*Crossly, to* WONG] Be off with you, rascal! [*He returns to his shop.*]

[SHEN TE *comes back out of the carpet shop with the* OLD MAN, *its proprietor, and his wife – whom we have already met – the* OLD WOMAN. SHEN TE *is wearing a shawl. The* OLD MAN *is holding up a looking-glass for her.*]

OLD WOMAN: Isn't it lovely? We'll give you a reduction because there's a little hole in it.

SHEN TE [*looking at another shawl on the* OLD WOMAN'S *arm*]: The other one's nice too.

OLD WOMAN [*smiling*]: Too bad there's no hole in that!

SHEN TE: That's right. My shop doesn't make very much.

OLD WOMAN: And your good deeds eat it all up! Be more careful, my dear. . . .

SHEN TE [*trying on the shawl with the hole*]: Just now, I'm lightheaded! Does the colour suit me?

OLD WOMAN: You'd better ask a man.

SHEN TE [*to the* OLD MAN]: Does the colour suit me?

OLD MAN: You'd better ask your young friend.

SHEN TE: I'd like to have your opinion.

OLD MAN: It suits you very well. But wear it this way: the dull side out.

[SHEN TE *pays up.*]

OLD WOMAN: If you decide you don't like it, you can exchange it. [*She pulls* SHEN TE *to one side.*] Has he got money?

SHEN TE [*with a laugh*]: Yang Sun? Oh, no.

OLD WOMAN: Then how're you going to pay your rent?

SHEN TE: I'd forgotten about that.

OLD WOMAN: And next Monday is the first of the month! Miss Shen Te, I've got something to say to you. After we [*indicating her husband*] got to know you, we had our doubts about that marriage ad. We thought it would be better if you'd let *us* help you. Out of our savings. We reckon we could lend you two hundred silver dollars. We don't need anything in writing – you could pledge us your tobacco stock.

SHEN TE: You're prepared to lend money to a person like me?

OLD WOMAN: It's folks like you that need it. We'd think twice about lending anything to your cousin.

OLD MAN [*coming up*]: All settled, my dear?

SHEN TE: I wish the gods could have heard what your wife was just saying, Mr Ma. They're looking for good people who're happy – and helping me makes you happy because you know it was love that got me into difficulties!

[*The* OLD COUPLE *smile knowingly at each other.*]

OLD MAN: And here's the money, Miss Shen Te. [*He hands her an envelope.* SHEN TE *takes it. She bows. They bow back. They return to their shop.*]

SHEN TE [*holding up her envelope*]: Look, Wong, here's six months' rent! Don't you believe in miracles now? And how do you like my new shawl?

WONG: For the young fellow I saw you with in the park? [SHEN TE *nods.*]

MRS SHIN: Never mind all that. It's time you took a look at his hand!

SHEN TE: Have you hurt your hand?

MRS SHIN: That barber smashed it with his hot curling iron. Right in front of our eyes.

SHEN TE [*shocked at herself*]: And I never noticed! We must get you to a doctor this minute or who knows what will happen?

UNEMPLOYED MAN: It's not a doctor he should see, it's a judge. He can ask for compensation. The barber's filthy rich.

WONG: You think I have a chance?

MRS SHIN [*with relish*]: If it's really good and smashed. But is it?

WONG: I think so. It's very swollen. Could I get a pension?

MRS SHIN: You'd need a witness.

WONG: Well, you all saw it. You could all testify. [*He looks round.*]

[*The* UNEMPLOYED MAN, *the* GRANDFATHER, *and the* SISTER-IN-LAW *are all sitting against the wall of the shop eating rice. Their concentration on eating is complete.*]

SHEN TE [*to* MRS SHIN]: You saw it yourself.

MRS SHIN: I want nothing to do with the police. It's against my principles.

SHEN TE [*to* SISTER-IN-LAW]: What about you?

SISTER-IN-LAW: Me? I wasn't looking.

SHEN TE [*to the* GRANDFATHER, *coaxingly*]: Grandfather, *you'll* testify, won't you?

SISTER-IN-LAW: And a lot of good that will do. He's simple-minded.

SHEN TE [*to the* UNEMPLOYED MAN]: You seem to be the only witness left.

UNEMPLOYED MAN: My testimony would only hurt him. I've been picked up twice for begging.

SHEN TE:

> Your brother is assaulted, and you shut your eyes?
> He is hit, cries out in pain, and you are silent?
> The beast prowls, chooses and seizes his victim, and you say:
> 'Because we showed no displeasure, he has spared us.'
> If no one present will be a witness, I will. I'll say *I* saw it.

MRS SHIN [*solemnly*]: The name for that is perjury.

WONG: I don't know if I can accept that. Though maybe I'll have to. [*Looking at his hand*] Is it swollen enough, do you think? The swelling's not going down?

UNEMPLOYED MAN: No, no, the swelling's holding up well.

WONG: Yes. It's *more* swollen if anything. Maybe my wrist is broken after all. I'd better see a judge at once. [*Holding his hand very carefully, and fixing his eyes on it, he runs off.*]

[MRS SHIN *goes quickly into the barber's shop.*]

UNEMPLOYED MAN [seeing her]: She is getting on the right side of Mr Shu Fu.

SISTER-IN-LAW: You and I can't change the world, Shen Te.

SHEN TE: Go away! Go away all of you! [The UNEMPLOYED MAN, the SISTER-IN-LAW, and the GRANDFATHER stalk off, eating and sulking. To the audience]

> They've stopped answering
> They stay put
> They do as they're told
> They don't care
> Nothing can make them look up
> But the smell of food.

[Enter MRS YANG, Yang Sun's mother, out of breath.]

MRS YANG: Miss Shen Te. My son has told me everything. I am Mrs Yang, Sun's mother. Just think. He's got an offer. Of a job as a pilot. A letter has just come. From the director of the airfield in Peking!

SHEN TE: So he can fly again? Isn't that wonderful!

MRS YANG [less breathlessly all the time]: They won't give him the job for nothing. They want five hundred silver dollars.

SHEN TE: We can't let money stand in his way, Mrs Yang!

MRS YANG: If only you could help him out!

SHEN TE: I have the shop. I can try! [She embraces MRS YANG.] I happen to have two hundred with me now. Take it. [She gives her the old couple's money.] It was a loan but they said I could repay it with my tobacco stock.

MRS YANG: And they were calling Sun the Dead Pilot of Set-zuan! A friend in need!

SHEN TE: We must find another three hundred.

MRS YANG: How?

SHEN TE: Let me think. [Slowly] I know someone who can help. I didn't want to call on his services again, he's hard and cunning. But a flyer must fly. And I'll make this the last time.

[Distant sound of a plane.]

MRS YANG: If the man you mentioned can do it.... Oh, look,
there's the morning mail plane, heading for Peking!

SHEN TE: The pilot can see us, let's wave!

[*They wave. The noise of the engine is louder.*]

MRS YANG: You know that pilot up there?

SHEN TE: Wave, Mrs Yang! I know the pilot who will be up
there. He gave up hope. But he'll do it now. One man to
raise himself above the misery, above us all. [*To the audience*]

> Yang Sun, my lover:
> Braving the storms
> In company with the clouds
> Crossing the heavens
> And bringing to friends in faraway lands
> The friendly mail!

4a

In front of the inner curtain. Enter SHEN TE, *carrying* SHUI TA'S
mask. She sings.

THE SONG OF DEFENCELESSNESS

> In our country
> A useful man needs luck
> Only if he finds strong backers
> Can he prove himself useful.
> The good can't defend themselves and
> Even the gods are defenceless.

> Oh, why don't the gods have their own ammunition
> And launch against badness their own expedition
> Enthroning the good and preventing sedition
> And bringing the world to a peaceful condition?

Oh, why don't the gods do the buying and selling
Injustice forbidding, starvation dispelling
Give bread to each city and joy to each dwelling?
Oh, why don't the gods do the buying and selling?

[*She puts on* SHUI TA's *mask and sings in his voice.*]

You can only help one of your luckless brothers
By trampling down a dozen others.

Why is it the gods do not feel indignation
And come down in fury to end exploitation
Defeat all defeat and forbid desperation
Refusing to tolerate such toleration?
Why is it?

5

Shen Te's tobacco shop. Behind the counter, MR SHUI TA, *reading the paper.* MRS SHIN *is cleaning up. She talks and he takes no notice.*

MRS SHIN: And when certain rumours get about, what *happens* to a little place like this? It goes to pot. *I* know. So, if you want my advice, Mr Shui Ta, find out just what has been going on between Miss Shen Te and that Yang Sun from Yellow Street. And remember: a certain interest in Miss Shen Te has been expressed by the barber next door, a man with twelve houses and only one wife, who, for that matter, is likely to drop off at any time. A certain interest has been expressed. He was even inquiring about her means and, if *that* doesn't prove a man is getting serious, what would? [*Still getting no response, she leaves with her bucket.*]
YANG SUN'S VOICE: Is that Miss Shen Te's tobacco shop?

MRS SHIN'S VOICE: Yes, it is, but it's Mr Shui Ta who's here today.

[SHUI TA *runs to the mirror with the short, light steps of* SHEN TE, *and is just about to start primping, when he realizes his mistake, and turns away, with a short laugh. Enter* YANG SUN. MRS SHIN *enters behind him and slips into the back room to eavesdrop.*]

YANG SUN: I am Yang Sun. [SHUI TA *bows.*] Is Shen Te in?

SHUI TA: No.

YANG SUN: I guess you know our relationship? [*He is inspecting the stock.*] Quite a place! And I thought she was just talking big. I'll be flying again, all right. [*He takes a cigar, solicits and receives a light from* SHUI TA.] You think we can squeeze the other three hundred out of the tobacco stock?

SHUI TA: May I ask if it is your intention to sell at once?

YANG SUN: It was decent of her to come out with the two hundred but they aren't much use with the other three hundred still missing.

SHUI TA: Shen Te was overhasty promising so much. She might have to sell the shop itself to raise it. Haste, they say, is the wind that blows the house down.

YANG SUN: Oh, she isn't a girl to keep a man waiting. For one thing or the other, if you take my meaning.

SHUI TA: I take your meaning.

YANG SUN [*leering*]: Uh, huh.

SHUI TA: Would you explain what the five hundred silver dollars are for?

YANG SUN: Want to sound me out? Very well. The director of the Peking airfield is a friend of mine from flying school. I give him five hundred: he gets me the job.

SHUI TA: The price is high.

YANG SUN: Not as these things go. He'll have to fire one of the present pilots – for negligence. Only the man he has in mind isn't negligent. Not easy, you understand. You needn't mention that part of it to Shen Te.

SHUI TA [*looking intently at* YANG SUN]: Mr Yang Sun, you are asking my cousin to give up her possessions, leave her friends, and place her entire fate in your hands. I presume you intend to marry her?

YANG SUN: I'd be prepared to.

[*Slight pause.*]

SHUI TA: Those two hundred silver dollars would pay the rent here for six months. If you were Shen Te wouldn't you be tempted to continue in business?

YANG SUN: What? Can you imagine Yang Sun the flyer behind a counter? [*In an oily voice*] 'A strong cigar or a mild one, worthy sir?' Not in this century!

SHUI TA: My cousin wishes to follow the promptings of her heart, and, from her own point of view, she may even have what is called the right to love. Accordingly, she has commissioned me to help you to this post. There is nothing here that I am not empowered to turn immediately into cash. Mrs Mi Tzu, the landlady, will advise me about the sale.

[*Enter* MRS MI TZU.]

MRS MI TZU: Good morning, Mr Shui Ta, you wish to see me about the rent? As you know it falls due the day after tomorrow.

SHUI TA: Circumstances have changed, Mrs Mi Tzu: my cousin is getting married. Her future husband here, Mr Yang Sun, will be taking her to Peking. I am interested in selling the tobacco stock.

MRS MI TZU: How much are you asking, Mr Shui Ta?

YANG SUN: Three hundred sil –

SHUI TA: Five hundred silver dollars.

MRS MI TZU: How much did she pay for it, Mr Shui Ta?

SHUI TA: A thousand. And very little has been sold.

MRS MI TZU: She was robbed. But I'll make you a special offer if you'll promise to be out by the day after tomorrow. Three hundred silver dollars.

YANG SUN [*shrugging*]: Take it, man, take it.

SHUI TA: It is not enough.

YANG SUN: Why not? Why not? Certainly, it's enough.

SHUI TA: Five hundred silver dollars.

YANG SUN: But why? We only need three!

SHUI TA [to MRS MI TZU]: Excuse me. [Takes YANG SUN on one side.] The tobacco stock is pledged to the old couple who gave my cousin the two hundred.

YANG SUN: Is it in writing?

SHUI TA: No.

YANG SUN [to MRS MI TZU]: Three hundred will do.

MRS MI TZU: Of course, I need an assurance that Miss Shen Te is not in debt.

YANG SUN: Mr Shui Ta?

SHUI TA: She is not in debt.

YANG SUN: When can you let us have the money?

MRS MI TZU: The day after tomorrow. And remember. I'm doing this because I have a soft spot in my heart for young lovers! [Exit.]

YANG SUN [calling after her]: Boxes, jars and sacks – three hundred for the lot and the pain's over! [To SHUI TA] Where else can we raise money by the day after tomorrow?

SHUI TA: Nowhere. Haven't you enough for the trip and the first few weeks?

YANG SUN: Oh, certainly.

SHUI TA: How much, exactly?

YANG SUN: Oh, I'll dig it up, even if I have to steal it.

SHUI TA: I see.

YANG SUN: Well, don't fall off the roof. I'll get to Peking somehow.

SHUI TA: Two people can't travel for nothing.

YANG SUN [not giving SHUI TA a chance to answer]: I'm leaving her behind. No millstones round my neck!

SHUI TA: Oh.

YANG SUN: Don't look at me like that!

SHUI TA: How precisely is my cousin to live?

YANG SUN: Oh, you'll think of something.

SHUI TA: A small request, Mr Yang Sun. Leave the two hundred silver dollars here until you can show me two tickets for Peking.

YANG SUN: You learn to mind your own business, Mr Shui Ta.

SHUI TA: I'm afraid Miss Shen Te may not wish to sell the shop when she discovers that . . .

YANG SUN: You don't know women. She'll want to. Even then.

SHUI TA [a slight outburst]: She is a human being, sir! And not devoid of common sense!

YANG SUN: Shen Te is a woman: she *is* devoid of common sense. I only have to lay my hand on her shoulder, and church bells ring.

SHUI TA [with difficulty]: Mr Yang Sun!

YANG SUN: Mr Shui Whatever-it-is!

SHUI TA: My cousin is devoted to you . . . because . . .

YANG SUN: Because I have my hands on her breasts. Give me a cigar. [He takes one for himself, stuffs a few more in his pocket, then changes his mind and takes the whole box.] Tell her I'll marry her, then bring me the three hundred. Or let her bring it. One or the other. [Exit.]

MRS SHIN [sticking her head out of the back room]: Well, he has your cousin under his thumb, and doesn't care if all Yellow Street knows it!

SHUI TA [crying out]: I've lost my shop! And he doesn't love me! [He runs berserk through the room, repeating these lines incoherently. Then stops suddenly, and addresses MRS SHIN.] Mrs Shin, you grew up in the gutter, like me. Are we lacking in hardness? I doubt it. If you steal a penny from me, I'll take you by the throat till you spit it out! You'd do the same to me. The times are bad, this city is hell, but we're like ants, we keep coming, up and up the walls, however smooth! Till bad luck comes. Being in love, for instance. One weakness is enough, and love is the deadliest.

MRS SHIN [*emerging from the back room*]: You should have a little talk with Mr Shu Fu, the barber. He's a real gentleman and just the thing for your cousin. [*She runs off.*]

SHUI TA:

A caress becomes a stranglehold
A sigh of love turns to a cry of fear
Why are there vultures circling in the air?
A girl is going to meet her lover.

[SHUI TA *sits down and* MR SHU FU *enters with* MRS SHIN.]

SHUI TA: Mr Shu Fu?

SHU FU: Mr Shui Ta.

[*They both bow.*]

SHUI TA: I am told that you have expressed a certain interest in my cousin Shen Te. Let me set aside all propriety and confess: she is at this moment in grave danger.

SHU FU: Oh, dear!

SHUI TA: She has lost her shop, Mr Shu Fu.

SHU FU: The charm of Miss Shen Te, Mr Shui Ta, derives from the goodness, not of her shop, but of her heart. Men call her the Angel of the Slums.

SHUI TA: Yet her goodness has cost her two hundred silver dollars in a single day: we must put a stop to it.

SHU FU: Permit me to differ, Mr Shui Ta. Let us, rather, open wide the gates to such goodness! Every morning, with pleasure tinged by affection, I watch her charitable ministrations. For they are hungry, and she giveth them to eat! Four of them, to be precise. Why only four? I ask. Why not four hundred? I hear she has been seeking shelter for the homeless. What about my humble cabins behind the cattle run? They are at her disposal. And so forth. And so on. Mr Shui Ta, do you think Miss Shen Te could be persuaded to listen to certain ideas of mine? Ideas like these?

SHUI TA: Mr Shu Fu, she would be honoured.

[*Enter* WONG *and the* POLICEMAN. MR SHU FU *turns abruptly away and studies the shelves.*]

WONG: Is Miss Shen Te here?

SHUI TA: No.

WONG: I am Wong the water seller. You are Mr Shui Ta?

SHUI TA: I am.

WONG: I am a friend of Shen Te's.

SHUI TA: An intimate friend, I hear.

WONG [to the POLICEMAN]: You see? [To SHUI TA] It's because of my hand.

POLICEMAN: He hurt his hand, sir, that's a fact.

SHUI TA [quickly]: You need a sling, I see. [He takes a shawl from the back room, and throws it to WONG.]

WONG: But that's her new shawl!

SHUI TA: She has no more use for it.

WONG: But she bought it to please someone!

SHUI TA: It happens to be no longer necessary.

WONG [making the sling]: She is my only witness.

POLICEMAN: Mr Shui Ta, your cousin is supposed to have seen the barber hit the water seller with a curling iron.

SHUI TA: I'm afraid my cousin was not present at the time.

WONG: But she was, sir! Just ask her! Isn't she in?

SHUI TA [gravely]: Mr Wong, my cousin has her own troubles. You wouldn't wish her to add to them by committing perjury?

WONG: But it was she that told me to go to the judge!

SHUI TA: Was the judge supposed to heal your hand?

[MR SHU FU turns quickly around. SHUI TA bows to SHU FU, and vice versa.]

WONG [taking the sling off, and putting it back]: I see how it is.

POLICEMAN: Well, I'll be on my way. [To WONG] And you be careful. If Mr Shu Fu wasn't a man who tempers justice with mercy, as the saying is, you'd be in jail for libel. Be off with you!

[Exit WONG, followed by POLICEMAN.]

SHUI TA: Profound apologies, Mr Shu Fu.

SHU FU: Not at all, Mr Shui Ta. [*Pointing to the shawl*] The episode is over?

SHUI TA: It may take her time to recover. There are some fresh wounds.

SHU FU: We shall be discreet. Delicate. A short vacation could be arranged. . . .

SHUI TA: First of course, you and she would have to talk things over.

SHU FU: At a small supper in a small, but high-class, restaurant.

SHUI TA: I'll go and find her. [*Exit into back room.*]

MRS SHIN [*sticking her head in again*]: Time for congratulations, Mr Shu Fu?

SHU FU: Ah, Mrs Shin! Please inform Miss Shen Te's guests they may take shelter in the cabins behind the cattle run!
[MRS SHIN *nods, grinning.*]

SHU FU [*to the audience*]: Well? What do you think of me, ladies and gentlemen? What could man do more? Could he be less selfish? More far-sighted? A small supper in a small but. . . . Does that bring rather vulgar and clumsy thoughts into your mind? Ts, ts, ts. Nothing of the sort will occur. She won't even be touched. Not even accidentally while passing the salt. An exchange of ideas only. Over the flowers on the table – white chrysanthemums, by the way [*he writes down a note of this*] – yes, over the white chrysanthemums, two young souls will . . . shall I say 'find each other'? We shall NOT exploit the misfortune of others. Understanding? Yes. An offer of assistance? Certainly. But quietly. Almost inaudibly. Perhaps with a single glance. A glance that could also – mean more.

MRS SHIN [*coming forward*]: Everything under control, Mr Shu Fu?

SHU FU: Oh, Mrs Shin, what do you know about this worthless rascal Yang Sun?

MRS SHIN: Why, he's the most worthless rascal . . .

SHU FU: Is he really? You're sure? [*As she opens her mouth*]

From now on, he doesn't exist! Can't be found anywhere!
[*Enter* YANG SUN.]

MRS SHIN: Shall I call Mr Shui Ta, Mr Shu Fu? He wouldn't want strangers in here!

SHU FU: Mr Shui Ta is in conference with Miss Shen Te. Not to be disturbed!

YANG SUN: Shen Te here? I didn't see her come in. What kind of conference?

SHU FU [*not letting him enter the back room*]: Patience, dear sir! And if by chance I have an inkling who you are, pray take note that Miss Shen Te and I are about to announce our engagement.

YANG SUN: What?

MRS SHIN: You didn't expect that, did you?

[YANG SUN *is trying to push past the barber into the back room when* SHEN TE *comes out.*]

SHU FU: My dear Shen Te, ten thousand apologies! Perhaps you . . .

YANG SUN: What is it, Shen Te? Have you gone crazy?

SHEN TE [*breathless*]: My cousin and Mr Shu Fu have come to an understanding. They wish me to hear Mr Shu Fu's plans for helping the poor.

YANG SUN: Your cousin wants to part us.

SHEN TE: Yes.

YANG SUN: And you've agreed to it?

SHEN TE: Yes.

YANG SUN: They told you I was bad. [SHEN TE *is silent.*] And suppose I am. Does that make me need you less? I'm low, Shen Te, I have no money, I don't do the right thing but at least I put up a fight! [*He is near her now, and speaks in an undertone.*] Have you no eyes? Look at him. Have you forgotten already?

SHEN TE: No.

YANG SUN: How it was raining?

SHEN TE: No.

YANG SUN: How you cut me down from the willow tree? Bought me water? Promised me money to fly with?

SHEN TE [*shakily*]: Yang Sun, what do you want?

YANG SUN: I want you to come with me.

SHEN TE [*in a small voice*]: Forgive me, Mr Shu Fu, I want to go with Mr Yang Sun.

YANG SUN: We're lovers you know. Give me the key to the shop. [SHEN TE *takes the key from around her neck.* YANG SUN *puts it on the counter. To* MRS SHIN] Leave it under the mat when you're through. Let's go, Shen Te.

SHU FU: But this is rape! Mr Shui Ta!!

YANG SUN [*to* SHEN TE]: Tell him not to shout.

SHEN TE: Please don't shout for my cousin, Mr Shu Fu. He doesn't agree with me, I know, but he's wrong. [*To the audience*]

> I want to go with the man I love
> I don't want to count the cost
> I don't want to consider if it's wise
> I don't want to know if he loves me
> I want to go with the man I love.

YANG SUN: That's the spirit.

[*And the couple leave.*]

5a

In front of the inner curtain. SHEN TE *in her wedding clothes, on the way to her wedding.*

SHEN TE: Something terrible has happened. As I left the shop with Yang Sun, I found the old carpet dealer's wife waiting on the street, trembling all over. She told me her husband had taken to his bed – sick with all the worry and excitement over the two hundred silver dollars they lent me. She said

it would be best if I gave it back now. Of course, I had to
say I would. She said she couldn't quite trust my cousin Shui
Ta or even my fiancé Yang Sun. There were tears in her
eyes. With my emotions in an uproar, I threw myself into
Yang Sun's arms, I couldn't resist him. The things he'd said
to Shui Ta had taught Shen Te nothing. Sinking into his
arms, I said to myself:

> To let no one perish, not even oneself
> To fill everyone with happiness, even oneself
> Is so good.

How could I have forgotten those two old people? Yang
Sun swept me away like a small hurricane. But he's not a
bad man, and he loves me. He'd rather work in the cement
factory than owe his flying to a crime. Though, of course,
flying *is* a great passion with Sun. Now, on the way to my
wedding, I waver between fear and joy.

6

*The 'private dining-room' on the upper floor of a cheap restaurant
in a poor section of town. With* SHEN TE: *the* GRANDFATHER,
the SISTER-IN-LAW, *the* NIECE, MRS SHIN, *the* UNEMPLOYED
MAN. *In a corner, alone, a* PRIEST. *A* WAITER *pouring wine.
Downstage,* YANG SUN *talking to his* MOTHER. *He wears a dinner
jacket.*

YANG SUN: Bad news, Mamma. She came right out and told
me she can't sell the shop for me. Some idiot is bringing a
claim because he lent her the two hundred she gave you.

MRS YANG: What did you say? Of course, you can't marry
her now.

YANG SUN: It's no use saying anything to *her*. I've sent for her
cousin, Mr Shui Ta. He said there was nothing in writing.

MRS YANG: Good idea. I'll go out and look for him. Keep an eye on things. [*Exit* MRS YANG.]

[SHEN TE *has been pouring wine.*]

SHEN TE [*to the audience, pitcher in hand*]: I wasn't mistaken in him. He's bearing up well. Though it must have been an awful blow – giving up flying. I do love him so. [*Calling across the room to him*] Sun, you haven't drunk a toast with the bride!

YANG SUN: What do we drink to?

SHEN TE: Why, to the future!

YANG SUN: When the bridegroom's dinner jacket won't be a hired one!

SHEN TE: But when the bride's dress will still get rained on sometimes!

YANG SUN: To everything we ever wished for!

SHEN TE: May all our dreams come true!

[*They drink.*]

YANG SUN [*with loud conviviality*]: And now, friends, before the wedding gets under way, I have to ask the bride a few questions. I've no idea what kind of a wife she'll make, and it worries me. [*Wheeling on* SHEN TE] For example. Can you make five cups of tea with three tea leaves?

SHEN TE: No.

YANG SUN: So I won't be getting very much tea. Can you sleep on a straw mattress the size of that book? [*He points to the large volume the* PRIEST *is reading.*]

SHEN TE: The two of us?

YANG SUN: The one of you.

SHEN TE: In that case, no.

YANG SUN: What a wife! I'm shocked!

[*While the audience is laughing, his* MOTHER *returns. With a shrug of her shoulders, she tells* SUN *the expected guest hasn't arrived. The* PRIEST *shuts the book with a bang, and makes for the door.*]

MRS YANG: Where are *you* off to? It's only a matter of minutes.

PRIEST [*watch in hand*]: Time goes on, Mrs Yang, and I've another wedding to attend to. Also a funeral.

MRS YANG [*irately*]: D'you think we planned it this way? I was hoping to manage with one pitcher of wine, and we've run through two already. [*Points to empty pitcher. Loudly*] My dear Shen Te, I don't know where your cousin can be keeping himself!

SHEN TE: My cousin? !

MRS YANG: Certainly. I'm old-fashioned enough to think such a close relative should attend the wedding.

SHEN TE: Oh, Sun, is it the three hundred silver dollars?

YANG SUN [*not looking her in the eye*]: Are you deaf? Mother says she's old-fashioned. And I say I'm considerate. We'll wait another fifteen minutes.

HUSBAND: Another fifteen minutes.

MRS YANG [*addressing the company*]: Now you all know, don't you, that my son is getting a job as a mail pilot?

SISTER-IN-LAW: In Peking, too, isn't it?

MRS YANG: In Peking, too! The two of us are moving to Peking!

SHEN TE: Sun, tell your mother Peking is out of the question now.

YANG SUN: Your cousin'll tell her. If he agrees. I don't agree.

SHEN TE [*amazed, and dismayed*]: Sun!

YANG SUN: I hate this godforsaken Setzuan. What people! Know what they look like when I half close my eyes? Horses! Whinnying, fretting, stamping, screwing their necks up! [*Loudly*] And what is it the thunder says? They are su-per-flu-ous! [*He hammers out the syllables.*] They've run their last race! They can go trample themselves to death! [*Pause.*] I've got to get out of here.

SHEN TE: But I've promised the money to the old couple.

YANG SUN: And since you always do the wrong thing, it's lucky your cousin's coming. Have another drink.

SHEN TE [*quietly*]: My cousin can't be coming.

YANG SUN: How d'you mean?

SHEN TE: My cousin can't be where I am.

YANG SUN: Quite a conundrum!

SHEN TE [*desperately*]: Sun, I'm the one that loves you. Not my cousin. He was thinking of the job in Peking when he promised you the old couple's money –

YANG SUN: Right. And that's why he's bringing the three hundred silver dollars. Here – to my wedding.

SHEN TE: He is not bringing the three hundred silver dollars.

YANG SUN: Huh? What makes you think that?

SHEN TE [*looking into his eyes*]: He says you only bought one ticket to Peking.

[*Short pause.*]

YANG SUN: That was yesterday. [*He pulls two tickets part way out of his inside pocket, making her look under his coat.*] Two tickets. I don't want Mother to know. She'll get left behind. I sold her furniture to buy these tickets, so you see . . .

SHEN TE: But what's to become of the old couple?

YANG SUN: What's to become of me? Have another drink. Or do you believe in moderation? If I drink, I fly again. And if you drink, you may learn to understand me.

SHEN TE: You want to fly. But I can't help you.

YANG SUN: 'Here's a plane, my darling – but it's only got one wing!'

[*The* WAITER *enters.*]

WAITER: Mrs Yang!

MRS YANG: Yes?

WAITER: Another pitcher of wine, ma'am?

MRS YANG: We have enough, thanks. Drinking makes me sweat.

WAITER: Would you mind paying, ma'am?

MRS YANG [*to everyone*]: Just be patient a few moments longer, everyone, Mr Shui Ta is on his way over! [*To the* WAITER] Don't be a spoil-sport.

WAITER: I can't let you leave till you've paid your bill, ma'am.

MRS YANG: But they know me here!

WAITER: That's just it.

PRIEST [*ponderously getting up*]: I humbly take my leave. [*And he does.*]

MRS YANG [*to the others, desperately*]: Stay where you are, everybody! The priest says he'll be back in two minutes!

YANG SUN: It's no good, Mamma. Ladies and gentlemen, Mr Shui Ta still hasn't arrived and the priest has gone home. We won't detain you any longer.

[*They are leaving now.*]

GRANDFATHER [*in the doorway, having forgotten to put his glass down*]: To the bride! [*He drinks, puts down the glass, and follows the others.*]

[*Pause.*]

SHEN TE: Shall I go too?

YANG SUN: You? Aren't you the bride? Isn't this your wedding? [*He drags her across the room, tearing her wedding dress.*] If we can wait, you can wait. Mother calls me her falcon. She wants to see me in the clouds. But I think it may be St Nevercome's Day before she'll go to the door and see my plane thunder by. [*Pause. He pretends the guests are still present.*] Why such a lull in the conversation, ladies and gentlemen? Don't you like it here? The ceremony is only slightly postponed – because an important guest is expected at any moment. Also because the bride doesn't know what love is. While we're waiting, the bridegroom will sing a little song. [*He does so.*]

THE SONG OF ST NEVERCOME'S DAY

On a certain day, as is generally known,
     One and all will be shouting: Hooray, hooray!
For the beggar maid's son has a solid-gold throne
     And the day is St Nevercome's Day
On St Nevercome's, Nevercome's, Nevercome's Day
     He'll sit on his solid-gold throne

Oh, hooray, hooray! That day goodness will pay!
  That day badness will cost you your head!
And merit and money will smile and be funny
  While exchanging salt and bread

On St Nevercome's, Nevercome's, Nevercome's Day
  While exchanging salt and bread
And the grass, oh, the grass will look down at the sky
  And the pebbles will roll up the stream
And all men will be good without batting an eye
  They will make of our earth a dream

On St Nevercome's, Nevercome's, Nevercome's Day
  They will make of our earth a dream
And as for me, that's the day I shall be
  A flyer and one of the best
Unemployed man, you will have work to do
  Washerwoman, you'll get your rest
On St Nevercome's, Nevercome's, Nevercome's Day
  Washerwoman, you'll get your rest

MRS YANG: It looks like he's not coming.
[*The three of them sit looking at the door.*]

6a

Wong's den. The sewer pipe is again transparent and again the GODS *appear to* WONG *in a dream.*

WONG: I'm so glad you've come, illustrious ones. It's Shen Te. She's in great trouble from following the rule about loving thy neighbour. Perhaps she's *too* good for this world!
FIRST GOD: Nonsense! You are eaten up by lice and doubts!
WONG: Forgive me, illustrious one, I only meant you might deign to intervene.

FIRST GOD: Out of the question! My colleague here intervened in some squabble or other only yesterday. [*He points to the* THIRD GOD *who has a black eye.*] The results are before us!

WONG: She had to call on her cousin again. But not even he could help. I'm afraid the shop is done for.

THIRD GOD [*a little concerned*]: Perhaps we should help after all?

FIRST GOD: The gods help those that help themselves.

WONG: What if we *can't* help ourselves, illustrious ones?
    [*Slight pause.*]

SECOND GOD: Try, anyway! Suffering ennobles!

FIRST GOD: Our faith in Shen Te is unshaken!

THIRD GOD: We certainly haven't found any *other* good people. You can see where we spend our nights from the straw on our clothes.

WONG: You might help her find her way by –

FIRST GOD: The good man finds his own way here below!

SECOND GOD: The good woman too.

FIRST GOD: The heavier the burden, the greater her strength!

THIRD GOD: We're only onlookers, you know.

FIRST GOD: And everything will be all right in the end, O ye of little faith!
    [*They are gradually disappearing through these last lines.*]

7

The yard behind Shen Te's shop. A few articles of furniture on a cart. SHEN TE *and* MRS SHIN *are taking the washing off the line.*

MRS SHIN: If you ask me, you should fight tooth and nail to keep the shop.

SHEN TE: How can I? I have to sell the tobacco to pay back the two hundred silver dollars today.

MRS SHIN: No husband, no tobacco, no house and home! What are you going to live on?

SHEN TE: I can work. I can sort tobacco.

MRS SHIN: Hey, look, Mr Shui Ta's trousers! He must have left here stark naked!

SHEN TE: Oh, he may have another pair, Mrs Shin.

MRS SHIN: But if he's gone for good as you say, why has he left his pants behind?

SHEN TE: Maybe he's thrown them away.

MRS SHIN: Can I take them?

SHEN TE: Oh, no.

[*Enter* MR SHU FU, *running.*]

SHU FU: Not a word! Total silence! I know all. You have sacrificed your own love and happiness so as not to hurt a dear old couple who had put their trust in you! Not in vain does this district – for all its malevolent tongues – call you the Angel of the Slums! That young man couldn't rise to your level, so you left him. And now, when I see you closing up the little shop, that veritable haven of rest for the multitude, well, I cannot, I cannot let it pass. Morning after morning I have stood watching in the doorway not unmoved – while you graciously handed out rice to the wretched. Is that never to happen again? Is the good woman of Setzuan to disappear? If only you would allow *me* to assist you! Now don't say anything! No assurances, no exclamations of gratitude! [*He has taken out his chequebook.*] Here! A blank cheque. [*He places it on the cart.*] Just my signature. Fill it out as you wish. Any sum in the world. I herewith retire from the scene, quietly, unobtrusively, making no claims, on tip-toe, full of veneration, absolutely selflessly . . . [*He has gone.*]

MRS SHIN: Well! You're saved. There's always some idiot of a man. . . . Now hurry! Put down a thousand silver dollars and let me fly to the bank before he comes to his senses.

SHEN TE: I can pay you for the washing without any cheque.

MRS SHIN: What? You're not going to cash it just because you might have to marry him? Are you crazy? Men like him *want* to be led by the nose! Are you still thinking of that flyer? All Yellow Street knows how he treated you!

SHEN TE:

When I heard his cunning laugh, I was afraid

But when I saw the holes in his shoes, I loved him dearly.

MRS SHIN: Defending that good-for-nothing after all that's happened!

SHEN TE [*staggering as she holds some of the washing*]: Oh!

MRS SHIN [*taking the washing from her, dryly*]: So you feel dizzy when you stretch and bend? There couldn't be a little visitor on the way? If that's it, you can forget Mr Shu Fu's blank cheque: it wasn't meant for a christening present! [*She goes to the back with a basket.*]

[SHEN TE'S *eyes follow* MRS SHIN *for a moment. Then she looks down at her own body, feels her stomach, and a great joy comes into her eyes.*]

SHEN TE: O joy! A new human being is on the way. The world awaits him. In the cities the people say: he's got to be reckoned with, this new human being! [*She imagines a little boy to be present, and introduces him to the audience.*] This is my son, the well-known flyer!

Say: Welcome

To the conqueror of unknown mountains and
    unreachable regions

Who brings us our mail across the impassable deserts!

[*She leads him up and down by the hand.*]

Take a look at the world, my son. That's a tree. Tree, yes. Say: 'Hello, tree!' And bow. Like this. [*She bows.*] Now you know each other. And, look, here comes the water seller. He's a friend, give him your hand. A cup of fresh water for my little son, please. Yes, it *is* a warm day. [*Handing the cup.*] Oh dear, a policeman, we'll have to make a circle round *him*. Perhaps we can pick a few cherries over there in the rich Mr Pung's garden. But we mustn't be seen.

You want cherries? Just like children with fathers. No, no, you can't go straight at them like that. Don't pull. We must learn to be reasonable. Well, have it your own way. [*She has let him make for the cherries.*] Can you reach? Where to put them? Your mouth is the best place. [*She tries one herself.*] Mmm, they're good. But the policeman, we must run! [*They run.*] Yes, back to the street. Calm now, so no one will notice us. [*Walking the street with her child, she sings.*]

>Once a plum – 'twas in Japan –
>Made a conquest of a man
>But the man's turn soon did come
>For he gobbled up the plum

[*Enter* WONG, *with a* CHILD *by the hand. He coughs.*]

SHEN TE: Wong!

WONG: It's about the carpenter, Shen Te. He's lost his shop, and he's been drinking. His children are on the streets. This is one. Can you help?

SHEN TE [*to the* CHILD]: Come here, little man. [*Takes him down to the footlights. To the audience*]

>You there! A man is asking you for shelter!
>A man of tomorrow says: what about today?
>His friend the conqueror, whom you know,
>Is his advocate!

[*To* WONG] He can live in Mr Shu Fu's cabins. I may have to go there myself. I'm going to have a baby. That's a secret – don't tell Yang Sun – we'd only be in his way. Can you find the carpenter for me?

WONG: I knew you'd think of something. [*To the* CHILD] Good-bye, son, I'm going for your father.

SHEN TE: What about your hand, Wong? I wanted to help, but my cousin ...

WONG: Oh, I can get along with one hand, don't worry. [*He shows how he can handle his pole with his left hand alone.*]

SHEN TE: But your right hand! Look, take this cart, sell everything that's on it, and go to the doctor with the money ...

WONG: She's still good. But first I'll bring the carpenter. I'll pick up the cart when I get back. [*Exit* WONG.]

SHEN TE [*to the* CHILD]: Sit down over here, son, till your father comes.

[*The* CHILD *sits cross-legged on the ground. Enter the* HUSBAND *and* WIFE, *each dragging a large, full sack.*]

WIFE [*furtively*]: You're alone, Shen Te, dear?

[SHEN TE *nods. The* WIFE *beckons to the* NEPHEW *offstage. He comes on with another sack.*]

WIFE: Your cousin's away? [SHEN TE *nods.*] He's not coming back?

SHEN TE: No. I'm giving up the shop.

WIFE: That's why we're here. We want to know if we can leave these things in your new home. Will you do us this favour?

SHEN TE: Why, yes, I'd be glad to.

HUSBAND [*cryptically*]: And if anyone asks about them, say they're yours.

SHEN TE: Would anyone ask?

WIFE [*with a glance back at her husband*]: Oh, someone might. The police, for instance. They don't seem to like us. Where can we put it?

SHEN TE: Well, I'd rather not get in any more trouble . . .

WIFE: Listen to her! The good woman of Setzuan!

[SHEN TE *is silent.*]

HUSBAND: There's enough tobacco in those sacks to give us a new start in life. We could have our own tobacco factory!

SHEN TE [*slowly*]: You'll have to put them in the back room.

[*The sacks are taken offstage, while the* CHILD *is alone. Shyly glancing about him, he goes to the garbage can, starts playing with the contents, and eating some of the scraps. The others return.*]

WIFE: We're counting on you, Shen Te!

SHEN TE: Yes. [*She sees the* CHILD *and is shocked.*]

HUSBAND: We'll see you in Mr Shu Fu's cabins.

NEPHEW: The day after tomorrow.

SHEN TE: Yes. Now, go. Go! I'm not feeling well.

[*Exeunt all three, virtually pushed off.*]

He is eating the refuse in the garbage can!
Only look at his little grey mouth!

[*Pause. Music.*]

As this is the world *my* son will enter
I will study to defend him.
To be good to you, my son,
I shall be a tigress to all others
If I have to.
And I shall have to.

[*She starts to go.*]

One more time, then. I hope really the last.

[*Exit SHEN TE, taking Shui Ta's trousers.*]

[MRS SHIN *enters and watches her with marked interest. Enter the* SISTER-IN-LAW *and the* GRANDFATHER.]

SISTER-IN-LAW: So it's true, the shop has closed down. And the furniture's in the back yard. It's the end of the road!

MRS SHIN [*pompously*]: The fruit of high living, selfishness, and sensuality! Down the primrose path to Mr Shu Fu's cabins – with you!

SISTER-IN-LAW: Cabins? Rat holes! He gave them to us because his soap supplies only went mouldy there!

[*Enter the* UNEMPLOYED MAN.]

UNEMPLOYED MAN: Shen Te is moving?

SISTER-IN-LAW: Yes. She was sneaking away.

MRS SHIN: She's ashamed of herself, and no wonder!

UNEMPLOYED MAN: Tell her to call Mr Shui Ta or she's done for this time!

SISTER-IN-LAW: Tell her to call Mr Shui Ta or *we're* done for this time!

[*Enter* WONG *and* CARPENTER, *the latter with a* CHILD *on each hand.*]

CARPENTER: So we'll have a roof over our heads for a change!

MRS SHIN: Roof? Whose roof?

CARPENTER: Mr Shu Fu's cabins. And we have little Feng to thank for it. [*Feng, we find, is the name of the* CHILD *already there; his* FATHER *now takes him. To the other* TWO] Bow to your little brother, you two!

    [*The* CARPENTER *and the* TWO NEW ARRIVALS *bow to* FENG.]

    [*Enter* SHUI TA.]

UNEMPLOYED MAN: Sst! Mr Shui Ta!

    [*Pause.*]

SHUI TA: And what is this crowd here for, may I ask?

WONG: How do you do, Mr Shui Ta. This is the carpenter. Miss Shen Te promised him space in Mr Shu Fu's cabins.

SHUI TA: That will not be possible.

CARPENTER: We can't go there after all?

SHUI TA: All the space is needed for other purposes.

SISTER-IN-LAW: You mean we have to get out? But we've got nowhere to go.

SHUI TA: Miss Shen Te finds it possible to provide employment. If the proposition interests you, you may stay in the cabins.

SISTER-IN-LAW [*with distaste*]: You mean *work*? Work for Miss Shen Te?

SHUI TA: Making tobacco, yes. There are three bales here already. Would you like to get them?

SISTER-IN-LAW [*trying to bluster*]: We have our own tobacco! We were in the tobacco business before you were born!

SHUI TA [*to the* CARPENTER *and the* UNEMPLOYED MAN]: You *don't* have your own tobacco. What about you?

    [*The* CARPENTER *and the* UNEMPLOYED MAN *get the point, and go for the sacks. Enter* MRS MI TZU.]

MRS MI TZU: Mr Shui Ta? I've brought you your three hundred silver dollars.

SHUI TA: I'll sign your lease instead. I've decided not to sell.

MRS MI TZU: What? You don't need the money for that flyer?

SHUI TA: No.

MRS MI TZU: And you can pay six months' rent?

SHUI TA [*takes the barber's blank cheque from the cart and fills it out*]: Here is a cheque for ten thousand silver dollars. On Mr Shu Fu's account. Look! [*He shows her the signature on the cheque.*] Your six months' rent will be in your hands by seven this evening. And now, if you'll excuse me.

MRS MI TZU: So it's Mr Shu Fu now. The flyer has been given his walking papers. These modern girls! In my day they'd have said she was flighty. That poor, deserted Mr Yang Sun! [*Exit* MRS MI TZU.]

[*The* CARPENTER *and the* UNEMPLOYED MAN *drag the three sacks back on the stage.*]

CARPENTER [*to* SHUI TA]: I don't know why I'm doing this for you.

SHUI TA: Perhaps your children want to eat, Mr Carpenter.

SISTER-IN-LAW [*catching sight of the sacks*]: Was my brother-in-law here?

MRS SHIN: Yes, he was.

SISTER-IN-LAW: I thought as much. I know those sacks! That's our tobacco!

SHUI TA: Really? I thought it came from my back room! Shall we consult the police on the point?

SISTER-IN-LAW [*defeated*]: No.

SHUI TA: Perhaps you will show me the way to Mr Shu Fu's cabins? [*Taking* FENG *by the hand,* SHUI TA *goes off, followed by the* CARPENTER *and his* TWO OLDER CHILDREN, *the* SISTER-IN-LAW, *the* GRANDFATHER, *and the* UNEMPLOYED MAN. *Each of the last three drags a sack.*]

[*Enter* OLD MAN *and* OLD WOMAN.]

MRS SHIN: A pair of pants – missing from the clothes line one minute – and next minute on the honourable backside of Mr Shui Ta.

OLD WOMAN: We thought Miss Shen Te was here.

MRS SHIN [*preoccupied*]: Well, she's not.

OLD MAN: There was something she was going to give us.

WONG: She was going to help me too. [*Looking at his hand*]
It'll be too late soon. But she'll be back. This cousin has
never stayed long.

MRS SHIN [*approaching a conclusion*]: No, he hasn't, has he?

7a

The sewer pipe: WONG *asleep. In his dreams, he tells the* GODS
his fears. The GODS *seem tired from all their travels. They stop for
a moment and look over their shoulders at the water seller.*

WONG: Illustrious ones. I've been having a bad dream. Our
beloved Shen Te was in great distress in the rushes down by
the river – the spot where the bodies of suicides are washed
up. She kept staggering and holding her head down as if she
was carrying something and it was dragging her down into
the mud. When I called out to her, she said she had to take
your Book of Rules to the other side, and not get it wet, or
the ink would all come off. You had talked to her about the
virtues, you know, the time she gave you shelter in Setzuan.

THIRD GOD: Well, but what do you suggest, my dear Wong?

WONG: Maybe a little relaxation of the rules, Benevolent One,
in view of the bad times.

THIRD GOD: As for instance?

WONG: Well, um, good-will, for instance, might do instead
of love?

THIRD GOD: I'm afraid that would create new problems.

WONG: Or, instead of justice, good sportsmanship?

THIRD GOD: That would only mean more work.

WONG: Instead of honour, outward propriety?

THIRD GOD: Still more work! No, no! The rules will have to
stand, my dear Wong!

[*Wearily shaking their heads, all three journey on.*]

8

Shui Ta's tobacco factory in Shu Fu's cabins. Huddled together behind bars, several FAMILIES, *mostly women and children. Among these people the* SISTER-IN-LAW, *the* GRANDFATHER, *the* CARPENTER, *and his* THREE CHILDREN. *Enter* MRS YANG *followed by* YANG SUN.

MRS YANG [*to the audience*]: There's something I just *have* to tell you: strength and wisdom are wonderful things. The strong and wise Mr Shui Ta has transformed my son from a dissipated good-for-nothing into a model citizen. As you may have heard, Mr Shui Ta opened a small tobacco factory near the cattle runs. It flourished. Three months ago – I shall never forget it – I asked for an appointment, and Mr Shui Ta agreed to see us – me and my son. I can see him now as he came through the door to meet us. ...

[*Enter* SHUI TA, *from a door.*]

SHUI TA: What can I do for you, Mrs Yang?

MRS YANG: This morning the police came to the house. We find you've brought an action for breach of promise of marriage. In the name of Shen Te. You also claim that Sun came by two hundred silver dollars by improper means.

SHUI TA: That is correct.

MRS YANG: Mr Shui Ta, the money's all gone. When the Peking job didn't materialize, he ran through it all in three days. I know he's a good-for-nothing. He sold my furniture. He was moving to Peking without me. Miss Shen Te thought highly of him at one time.

SHUI TA: What do *you* say, Mr Yang Sun?

YANG SUN: The money's gone.

SHUI TA [*to* MRS YANG]: Mrs Yang, in consideration of my cousin's incomprehensible weakness for your son, I am

prepared to give him another chance. He can have a job –
here. The two hundred silver dollars will be taken out of
his wages.

YANG SUN: So it's the factory or jail?

SHUI TA: Take your choice.

YANG SUN: May I speak with Shen Te?

SHUI TA: You may not.

[*Pause.*]

YANG SUN [*sullenly*]: Show me where to go.

MRS YANG: Mr Shui Ta, you are kindness itself: the gods will
reward you! [*To* YANG SUN] And honest work will make
a man of you, my boy. [YANG SUN *follows* SHUI TA *into the
factory.* MRS YANG *comes down again to the footlights.*] Actually, honest work didn't agree with him – at first. And he
got no opportunity to distinguish himself till – in the third
week – when the wages were being paid . . .

[SHUI TA *has a bag of money. Standing next to his foreman
– the former* UNEMPLOYED MAN *– he counts out the wages.
It is* YANG SUN'S *turn.*]

UNEMPLOYED MAN [*reading*]: Carpenter, six silver dollars.
Yang Sun, six silver dollars.

YANG SUN [*quietly*]: Excuse me, sir. I don't think it can be
more than five. May I see? [*He takes the foreman's list.*] It says
six working days. But that's a mistake, sir. I took a day off
for court business. And I won't take what I haven't earned,
however miserable the pay is!

UNEMPLOYED MAN: Yang Sun. Five silver dollars. [*To* SHUI
TA] A rare case, Mr Shui Ta!

SHUI TA: How is it the book says six when it should say five?

UNEMPLOYED MAN: I must've made a mistake, Mr Shui Ta.
[*With a look at* YANG SUN] It won't happen again.

SHUI TA [*taking* YANG SUN *aside*]: You don't hold back, do
you? You give your all to the firm. You're even honest.
Do the foreman's mistakes always favour the workers?

YANG SUN: He does have . . . friends.

SHUI TA: Thank you. May I offer you any little recompense?

YANG SUN: Give me a trial period of one week, and I'll prove my intelligence is worth more to you than my strength.

MRS YANG [*still down at the footlights*]: Fighting words, fighting words! That evening, I said to Sun: 'If you're a flyer, then fly, my falcon! Rise in the world!' And he got to be foreman. Yes, in Mr Shui Ta's tobacco factory, he worked real miracles.

[*We see* YANG SUN *with his legs apart standing behind the* WORKERS *who are handing along a basket of raw tobacco above their heads.*]

YANG SUN: Faster! Faster! You, there, d'you think you can just stand around, now you're not foreman any more? It'll be your job to lead us in song. Sing!

[UNEMPLOYED MAN *starts singing. The others join in the refrain.*]

SONG OF THE EIGHTH ELEPHANT

Chang had seven elephants – all much the same—
    But then there was Little Brother
The seven, they were wild, Little Brother, he was tame
    And to guard them Chang chose Little Brother
        Run faster!
        Mr Chang has a forest park
        Which must be cleared before tonight
        And already it's growing dark!

When the seven elephants cleared that forest park
    Mr Chang rode high on Little Brother
While the seven toiled and moiled till dark
    On his big behind sat Little Brother
        Dig faster!
        Mr Chang has a forest park
        Which must be cleared before tonight
        And already it's growing dark!

And the seven elephants worked many an hour
  Till none of them could work another
Old Chang, he looked sour, on the seven he did glower
  But gave a pound of rice to Little Brother
    What was that?
    Mr Chang has a forest park
    Which must be cleared before tonight
    And already it's growing dark!

And the seven elephants hadn't any tusks
  The one that had the tusks was Little Brother
Seven are no match for one, if the one has a gun!
  How old Chang did laugh at Little Brother!
    Keep on digging!
    Mr Chang has a forest park
    Which must be cleared before tonight
    And already it's growing dark!

[*Smoking a cigar,* SHUI TA *strolls by.* YANG SUN, *laughing, has joined in the refrain of the third stanza and speeded up the tempo of the last stanza by clapping his hands.*]

MRS YANG: And that's why I say: strength and wisdom are wonderful things. It took the strong and wise Mr Shui Ta to bring out the best in Yang Sun. A real superior man is like a bell. If you ring it, it rings, and if you don't, it don't, as the saying is.

9

Shen Te's shop, now an office with club chairs and fine carpets. It is raining. SHUI TA, *now fat, is just dismissing the* OLD MAN *and* OLD WOMAN. MRS SHIN, *in obviously new clothes, looks on, smirking.*

SHUI TA: No! I can NOT tell you when we expect her back.

OLD WOMAN: The two hundred silver dollars came today. In an envelope. There was no letter, but it must be from Shen Te. We want to write and thank her. May we have her address?

SHUI TA: I'm afraid I haven't got it.

OLD MAN [*pulling* OLD WOMAN'S *sleeve*]: Let's be going.

OLD WOMAN: She's got to come back some time! [*They move off, uncertainly, worried.*]

[SHUI TA *bows.*]

MRS SHIN: They lost the carpet shop because they couldn't pay their taxes. The money arrived too late.

SHUI TA: They could have come to me.

MRS SHIN: People don't like coming to you.

SHUI TA [*sits suddenly, one hand to his head*]: I'm dizzy.

MRS SHIN: After all, you *are* in your seventh month. But old Mrs Shin will be there in your hour of trial! [*She cackles feebly.*]

SHUI TA [*in a stifled voice*]: Can I count on that?

MRS SHIN: We all have our price, and mine won't be too high for the great Mr Shui Ta! [*She opens* SHUI TA'S *collar.*]

SHUI TA: It's for the child's sake. All of this.

MRS SHIN: 'All for the child', of course.

SHUI TA: I'm so fat. People must notice.

MRS SHIN: Oh no, they think it's 'cause you're rich.

SHUI TA [*more feelingly*]: What will happen to the child?

MRS SHIN: You ask that nine times a day. Why, it'll have the best that money can buy!

SHUI TA: He must never see Shui Ta.

MRS SHIN: Oh, no. Always Shen Te.

SHUI TA: What about the neighbours? There are rumours, aren't there?

MRS SHIN: As long as Mr Shu Fu doesn't find out, there's nothing to worry about. Drink this.

[*Enter* YANG SUN *in a smart business suit, and carrying a*

businessman's briefcase. SHUI TA *is more or less in* MRS
SHIN'S *arms.*]

YANG SUN [*surprised*]: I guess I'm in the way.

SHUI TA [*ignoring this, rises with an effort*]: Till tomorrow, Mrs
Shin.

[MRS SHIN *leaves with a smile, putting her new gloves on.*]

YANG SUN: Gloves now! She couldn't be fleecing you? And
since when did *you* have a private life? [*Taking a paper from
the briefcase*] You haven't been at your best lately, and things
are getting out of hand. The police want to close us down.
They say that at the most they can only permit twice the
lawful number of workers.

SHUI TA [*evasively*]: The cabins are quite good enough.

YANG SUN: For the workers maybe, not for the tobacco.
They're too damp. We must take over some of Mrs Mi
Tzu's buildings.

SHUI TA: Her price is double what I can pay.

YANG SUN: Not unconditionally. If she has me to stroke her
knees she'll come down.

SHUI TA: I'll never agree to that.

YANG SUN: What's wrong? Is it the rain? You get so irritable
whenever it rains.

SHUI TA: Never! I will never . . .

YANG SUN: Mrs Mi Tzu'll be here in five minutes. *You* fix it.
And Shu Fu will be with her. . . . What's all that noise?

[*During the above dialogue,* WONG *is heard offstage, calling:*
'The good Shen Te, where is she? Which of you has seen
Shen Te, good people? Where is Shen Te?' *A knock. Enter*
WONG.]

WONG: Mr Shui Ta, I've come to ask when Miss Shen Te will
be back, it's six months now. . . . There are rumours. People
say something's happened to her.

SHUI TA: I'm busy. Come back next week.

WONG [*excited*]: In the morning there was always rice on her
doorstep – for the needy. It's been there again lately!

SHUI TA: And what do people conclude from this?

WONG: That Shen Te is still in Setzuan! She's been . . . [*He breaks off.*]

SHUI TA: She's been what? Mr Wong, if you're Shen Te's friend, talk a little less about her, that's my advice to you.

WONG: I don't want your advice! Before she disappeared, Miss Shen Te told me something very important – she's pregnant!

YANG SUN: What? What was that?

SHUI TA [*quickly*]: The man is lying.

WONG: A good woman isn't so easily forgotten, Mr Shui Ta. [*He leaves.*]

[SHUI TA *goes quickly into the back room.*]

YANG SUN [*to the audience*]: Shen Te pregnant? So that's why. Her cousin sent her away, so I wouldn't get wind of it. I have a son, a Yang appears on the scene, and what happens? Mother and child vanish into thin air! That scoundrel, that unspeakable . . . [*The sound of sobbing is heard from the back room.*] What was that? Someone sobbing? Who was it? Mr Shui Ta the Tobacco King doesn't weep his heart out. And where does the rice come from that's on the doorstep in the morning? [SHUI TA *returns. He goes to the door and looks out into the rain.*] Where is she?

SHUI TA: Sh! It's nine o'clock. But the rain's so heavy, you can't hear a thing.

YANG SUN: What do you want to hear?

SHUI TA: The mail plane.

YANG SUN: What?!

SHUI TA: I've been told *you* wanted to fly at one time. Is that all forgotten?

YANG SUN: Flying mail is night work. I prefer the daytime. And the firm is very dear to me – after all it belongs to my ex-fiancée, even if she's not around. And she's not, is she?

SHUI TA: What do you mean by that?

YANG SUN: Oh, well, let's say I haven't altogether – lost interest.

SHUI TA: My cousin might like to know that.

YANG SUN: I might not be indifferent – if I found she was being kept under lock and key.

SHUI TA: By whom?

YANG SUN: By you.

SHUI TA: What could you do about it?

YANG SUN: I could submit for discussion – my position in the firm.

SHUI TA: You are now my manager. In return for a more ... appropriate position, you might agree to drop the inquiry into your ex-fiancée's whereabouts?

YANG SUN: I might.

SHUI TA: What position *would* be more appropriate?

YANG SUN: The one at the top.

SHUI TA: My own? [*Silence.*] And if I preferred to throw you out on your neck?

YANG SUN: I'd come back on my feet. With suitable escort.

SHUI TA: The police?

YANG SUN: The police.

SHUI TA: And when the police found no one?

YANG SUN: I might ask them not to overlook the back room. [*Ending the pretence*] In short, Mr Shui Ta, my interest in this young woman has not been officially terminated. I should like to see more of her. [*Into* SHUI TA's *face*] Besides, she's pregnant and needs a friend. [*He moves to the door.*] I shall talk about it with the water seller. [*Exit.*]

[SHUI TA *is rigid for a moment, then he quickly goes into the back room. He returns with Shen Te's belongings: underwear, etc. He takes a long look at the shawl of the previous scene. He then wraps the things in a bundle, which, upon hearing a noise, he hides under the table. Enter* MRS MI TZU *and* MR SHU FU. *They put away their umbrellas and galoshes.*]

MRS MI TZU: I thought your manager was here, Mr Shui Ta.

He combines charm with business in a way that can only be to the advantage of all of us.

SHU FU: You sent for us, Mr Shui Ta?

SHUI TA: The factory is in trouble.

SHU FU: It always is.

SHUI TA: The police are threatening to close us down unless I can show that the extension of our facilities is imminent.

SHU FU: Mr Shui Ta, I'm sick and tired of your constantly expanding projects. I place cabins at your cousin's disposal; you make a factory of them. I hand your cousin a cheque; you present it. Your cousin disappears: you find the cabins too small and start talking of yet more –

SHUI TA: Mr Shu Fu, I'm authorized to inform you that Miss Shen Te's return is now imminent.

SHU FU: Imminent? It's becoming his favourite word.

MRS MI TZU: Yes, what does it mean?

SHUI TA: Mrs Mi Tzu, I can pay you exactly half what you asked for your buildings. Are you ready to inform the police that I am taking them over?

MRS MI TZU: Certainly, if I can take over your manager.

SHU FU: What?

MRS MI TZU: He's so efficient.

SHUI TA: I'm afraid I need Mr Yang Sun.

MRS MI TZU: So do I.

SHUI TA: He will call on you tomorrow.

SHU FU: So much the better. With Shen Te likely to turn up at any moment, the presence of that young man is hardly in good taste.

SHUI TA: So we have reached a settlement. In what was once the good Shen Te's little shop we are laying the foundations for the great Mr Shui Ta's twelve magnificent super tobacco markets. You will bear in mind that though they call me the Tobacco King of Setzuan, it is my cousin's interests that have been served . . .

VOICES [*off*]: The police, the police! Going to the tobacco shop! Something must have happened!

[*Enter* YANG SUN, WONG, *and the* POLICEMAN.]

POLICEMAN: Quiet there, quiet, quiet! [*They quieten down.*] I'm sorry Mr Shui Ta, but there's a report that you've been depriving Miss Shen Te of her freedom. Not that I believe all I hear, but the whole city's in an uproar.

SHUI TA: That's a lie.

POLICEMAN: Mr Yang Sun has testified that he heard someone sobbing in the back room.

SHU FU: Mrs Mi Tzu and myself will testify that no one here has been sobbing.

MRS MI TZU: We have been quietly smoking our cigars.

POLICEMAN: Mr Shui Ta, I'm afraid I shall have to take a look at that room. [*He does so. The room is empty.*] No one there, of course, sir.

YANG SUN: But I heard sobbing. What's that? [*He finds the clothes.*]

WONG: Those are Shen Te's things. [*To crowd*] Shen Te's clothes are here!

VOICES [*off, in sequence*]: Shen Te's clothes!
– They've been found under the table!
– Body of murdered girl still missing!
– Tobacco King suspected!

POLICEMAN: Mr Shui Ta, unless you can tell us where the girl is, I'll have to ask you to come along.

SHUI TA: I do not know.

POLICEMAN: I can't say how sorry I am, Mr Shui Ta. [*He shows him the door.*]

SHUI TA: Everything will be cleared up in no time. There are still judges in Setzuan.

YANG SUN: I heard sobbing!

9a

Wong's den. For the last time, the GODS *appear to the water seller in his dream. They have changed and show signs of a long journey, extreme fatigue and, plenty of mishaps. The* FIRST *no longer has a hat; the* THIRD *has lost a leg; all three are barefoot.*

WONG: Illustrious ones, at last you're here. Shen Te's been gone for months and today her cousin's been arrested. They think he murdered her to get the shop. But I had a dream and in this dream Shen Te said her cousin was keeping her prisoner. You must find her for us, illustrious ones!

FIRST GOD: We've found very few good people anywhere, and even they didn't keep it up. Shen Te is still the only one that stayed good.

SECOND GOD: If she *has* stayed good.

WONG: Certainly she has. But she's vanished.

FIRST GOD: That's the last straw. All is lost!

SECOND GOD: A little moderation, dear colleague!

FIRST GOD [*plaintively*]: What's the good of moderation now? If she can't be found, we'll have to resign! The world is a terrible place! Nothing but misery, vulgarity, and waste! Even the countryside isn't what it used to be. The trees are getting their heads chopped off by telephone wires, and there's such a noise from all the gunfire, and I can't stand those heavy clouds of smoke, and –

THIRD GOD: The place is absolutely unlivable! Good intentions bring people to the brink of the abyss, and good deeds push them over the edge. I'm afraid our book of rules is destined for the scrap heap –

SECOND GOD: It's people! They're a worthless lot!

THIRD GOD: The world is too cold!

SECOND GOD: It's people! They're too weak!

FIRST GOD: Dignity, dear colleagues, dignity! Never despair! As for this world, didn't we agree that we only have to find one human being who can stand the place? Well, we found her. True, we lost her again. We must find her again, that's all! And at once!

[*They disappear.*]

10

Courtroom. Groups: SHU FU *and* MRS MI TZU; YANG SUN *and* MRS YANG; WONG, *the* CARPENTER, *the* GRANDFATHER, *the* NIECE, *the* OLD MAN, *the* OLD WOMAN; MRS SHIN, *the* POLICEMAN; *the* UNEMPLOYED MAN, *the* SISTER-IN-LAW.

OLD MAN: So much power isn't good for one man.

UNEMPLOYED MAN: And he's going to open twelve super tobacco markets!

WIFE: One of the judges is a friend of Mr Shu Fu's.

SISTER-IN-LAW: Another one accepted a present from Mr Shui Ta only last night. A great fat goose.

OLD WOMAN [*to* WONG]: And Shen Te is nowhere to be found.

WONG: Only the gods will ever know the truth.

POLICEMAN: Order in the court! My lords the judges!

[*Enter the* THREE GODS *in judges' robes. We overhear their conversation as they pass along the footlights to their bench.*]

THIRD GOD: We'll never get away with it, our certificates were so badly forged.

SECOND GOD: My predecessor's 'sudden indigestion' will certainly cause comment.

FIRST GOD: But he *had* just eaten a whole goose.

UNEMPLOYED MAN: Look at that! *New* judges.

WONG: New judges. And what good ones!

[*The* THIRD GOD *hears this, and turns to smile at* WONG. *The* GODS *sit. The* FIRST GOD *beats on the bench with his* gavel. *The* POLICEMAN *brings in* SHUI TA *who walks with lordly steps. He is whistled at.*]

POLICEMAN [*to* SHUI TA]: Be prepared for a surprise. The judges have been changed.

[SHUI TA *turns quickly round, looks at them, and staggers.*]

NIECE: What's the matter now?

WIFE: The great Tobacco King nearly fainted.

HUSBAND: Yes, as soon as he saw the new judges.

WONG: Does he know who they are?

[SHUI TA *picks himself up, and the proceedings open.*]

FIRST GOD: Defendant Shui Ta, you are accused of doing away with your cousin Shen Te in order to take possession of her business. Do you plead guilty or not guilty?

SHUI TA: Not guilty, my lord.

FIRST GOD [*thumbing through the documents of the case*]: The first witness is the policeman. I shall ask him to tell us something of the respective reputations of Miss Shen Te and Mr Shui Ta.

POLICEMAN: Miss Shen Te was a young lady who aimed to please, my lord. She liked to live and let live, as the saying goes. Mr Shui Ta, on the other hand, is a man of principle. Though the generosity of Miss Shen Te forced him at times to abandon half measures, unlike the girl he was always on the side of the law, my lord. One time, he even unmasked a gang of thieves to whom his too trustful cousin had given shelter. The evidence, in short, my lord, proves that Mr Shui Ta was *incapable* of the crime of which he stands accused!

FIRST GOD: I see. And are there others who could testify along, shall we say, the same lines?

[SHU FU *rises.*]

POLICEMAN [*whispering to* GODS]: Mr Shu Fu – a very important person.

FIRST GOD [*inviting him to speak*]: Mr Shu Fu!

SHU FU: Mr Shui Ta is a businessman, my lord. Need I say more?

FIRST GOD: Yes.

SHU FU: Very well. I will. He is Vice President of the Council of Commerce and is about to be elected a Justice of the Peace. [*He returns to his seat.*]

[MRS MI TZU *rises.*]

WONG. Elected! *He* gave him the job!

[*With a gesture the* FIRST GOD *asks who* MRS MI TZU *is.*]

POLICEMAN: Another very important person. Mrs Mi Tzu.

FIRST GOD [*inviting her to speak*]: Mrs Mi Tzu!

MRS MI TZU: My lord, as Chairman of the Committee on Social Work, I wish to call attention to just a couple of eloquent facts: Mr Shui Ta not only has erected a model factory with model housing in our city, he is a regular contributor to our home for the disabled. [*She returns to her seat.*]

POLICEMAN [*whispering*]: And she's a great friend of the judge that ate the goose!

FIRST GOD [*to the* POLICEMAN]: Oh, thank you. What next? [*To the Court, genially*] Oh, yes. We should find out if any of the evidence is less favourable to the defendant.

[WONG, *the* CARPENTER, *the* OLD MAN, *the* OLD WOMAN, *the* UNEMPLOYED MAN, *the* SISTER-IN-LAW, *and the* NIECE *come forward.*]

POLICEMAN [*whispering*]: Just the riff-raff, my lord.

FIRST GOD [*addressing the 'riff-raff'*]: Well, um, riff-raff – do you know anything of the defendant, Mr Shui Ta?

WONG: Too much, my lord.

UNEMPLOYED MAN: What don't we know, my lord.

CARPENTER: He ruined us.

SISTER-IN-LAW: He's a cheat.

NIECE: Liar.

WIFE: Thief.

BOY: Blackmailer.

BROTHER: Murderer.

FIRST GOD: Thank you. We should now let the defendant state his point of view.

SHUI TA: I only came on the scene when Shen Te was in danger of losing what I had understood was a gift from the gods. Because I did the filthy jobs which someone had to do, they hate me. My activities were restricted to the minimum, my lord.

SISTER-IN-LAW: He had us arrested!

SHUI TA: Certainly. You stole from the bakery!

SISTER-IN-LAW: Such concern for the bakery! You didn't want the shop for yourself, I suppose!

SHUI TA: I didn't want the shop overrun with parasites.

SISTER-IN-LAW: We had nowhere else to go.

SHUI TA: There were too many of you.

WONG: What about this old couple: Were *they* parasites?

OLD MAN: We lost our shop because of you!

OLD WOMAN: And we gave your cousin money!

SHUI TA: My cousin's fiancé was a flyer. The money had to go to *him*.

WONG: Did you care whether he flew or not? Did you care whether she married him or not? You wanted her to marry someone else! [*He points at* SHU FU.]

SHUI TA: The flyer unexpectedly turned out to be a scoundrel.

YANG SUN [*jumping up*]: Which was the reason you made him your manager?

SHUI TA: Later on he improved.

WONG: And when he improved, you sold him to her? [*He points out* MRS MI TZU.]

SHUI TA: She wouldn't let me have her premises unless she had him to stroke her knees!

MRS MI TZU: What? The man's a pathological liar. [*To him*] Don't mention my property to me as long as you live! Murderer! [*She rustles off, in high dudgeon.*]

YANG SUN [*pushing in*]: My lord, I wish to speak for the defendant.

SISTER-IN-LAW: Naturally. He's your employer.

UNEMPLOYED MAN: And the worst slave driver in the country.

MRS YANG: That's a lie! My lord, Mr Shui Ta is a great man. He . . .

YANG SUN: He's this and he's that, but he is not a murderer, my lord. Just fifteen minutes before his arrest I heard Shen Te's voice in his own back room.

FIRST GOD: Oh? Tell us more!

YANG SUN: I heard sobbing, my lord!

FIRST GOD: But lots of women sob, we've been finding.

YANG SUN: Could I fail to recognize her voice?

SHU FU: No, you made her sob so often yourself, young man!

YANG SUN: Yes. But I also made her happy. Till he [pointing at SHUI TA] decided to sell her to you!

SHUI TA: Because you didn't love her.

WONG: Oh, no: it was for the money, my lord!

SHUI TA: And what was the money for, my lord? For the poor! And for Shen Te so she could go on being good!

WONG: For the poor? That he sent to his sweatshops? And why didn't you let Shen Te be good when you signed the big cheque?

SHUI TA: For the child's sake, my lord.

CARPENTER: What about my children? What did he do about them?

[SHUI TA is silent.]

WONG: The shop was to be a fountain of goodness. That was the gods' idea. You came and spoiled it!

SHUI TA: If I hadn't, it would have run dry!

MRS SHIN: There's a lot in that, my lord.

WONG: What have you done with the good Shen Te, bad man? She was good, my lords, she was, I swear it! [He raises his hand in an oath.]

THIRD GOD: What's happened to your hand, water seller?

WONG [pointing to SHUI TA]: It's all his fault, my lord, she was going to send me to a doctor – [*To* SHUI TA] You were her worst enemy!

SHUI TA: I was her only friend!

WONG: Where is she then? Tell us where your good friend is! [*The excitement of this exchange has run through the whole crowd.*]

ALL: Yes, where is she? Where is Shen Te? [*Etc.*]

SHUI TA: Shen Te . . . had to go.

WONG: Where? Where to?

SHUI TA: I cannot tell you! I cannot tell you!

ALL: Why? Why did she have to go away? [*Etc.*]

WONG [*into the din with the first words, but talking on beyond the others*]: Why not, why not? Why did she have to go away?

SHUI TA [*shouting*]: Because you'd all have torn her to shreds, that's why! My lords, I have a request. Clear the court! When only the judges remain, I will make a confession.

ALL [*except* WONG, *who is silent, struck by the new turn of events*]: So he's guilty? He's confessing! [*Etc.*]

FIRST GOD [*using the gavel*]: Clear the court!

POLICEMAN: Clear the court!

WONG: Mr Shui Ta has met his match this time.

MRS SHIN [*with a gesture towards the judges*]: You're in for a little surprise.

[*The court is cleared. Silence.*]

SHUI TA: Illustrious ones!

[*The* GODS *look at each other, not quite believing their ears.*]

SHUI TA: Yes, I recognize you!

SECOND GOD [*taking matters in hand, sternly*]: What have you done with our good woman of Setzuan?

SHUI TA: I have a terrible confession to make: I am she! [*He takes off his mask, and tears away his clothes.* SHEN TE *stands there.*]

SECOND GOD: Shen Te!

SHEN TE: Shen Te, yes. Shui Ta *and* Shen Te. Both.

Your injunction
To be good and yet to live
Was a thunderbolt:
It has torn me in two
I can't tell how it was
But to be good to others
And myself at the same time
I could not do it
Your world is not an easy one, illustrious ones!
When we extend our hand to a beggar, he tears it
    off for us
When we help the lost, we are lost ourselves
And so
Since not to eat is to die
Who can long refuse to be bad?
As I lay prostrate beneath the weight of good
    intentions
Ruin stared me in the face
It was when I was unjust that I ate good meat
And hob-nobbed with the mighty
Why?
Why are bad deeds rewarded?
Good ones punished?
I enjoyed giving
I truly wished to be the Angel of the Slums
But washed by a foster-mother in the water of
    the gutter
I developed a sharp eye
The time came when pity was a thorn in my side
And, later, when kind words turned to ashes in
    my mouth
And anger took over
I became a wolf
Find me guilty, then, illustrious ones,
But know:

All that I have done I did
To help my neighbour
To love my lover
And to keep my little one from want
For your great, godly deeds, I was too poor, too
small.

[*Pause.*]

FIRST GOD [*shocked*]: Don't go on making yourself miserable, Shen Te! We're overjoyed to have found you!

SHEN TE: I'm telling you I'm the bad man who committed all those crimes!

FIRST GOD [*using – or failing to use – his ear trumpet*]: The good woman who did all those good deeds?

SHEN TE: Yes, but the bad man too!

FIRST GOD [*as if something had dawned*]: Unfortunate coincidences! Heartless neighbours!

THIRD GOD [*shouting in his ear*]: But how is she to continue?

FIRST GOD: Continue? Well, she's a strong, healthy girl . . .

SECOND GOD: You didn't hear what she said!

FIRST GOD: I heard every word! She is confused, that's all! [*He begins to bluster*] And what about this book of rules – we can't renounce our rules, can we? [*More quietly*] Should the world be changed? How? By whom? The world should *not* be changed! [*At a sign from him, the lights turn pink, and music plays.*]★

And now the hour of parting is at hand.
Dost thou behold, Shen Te, yon fleecy cloud?
It is our chariot. At a sign from me
'Twill come and take us back from whence we
came
Above the azure vault and silver stars. . . .

★ The rest of this scene has been adapted for the many theatres that do not have 'fly-space' to lower things from on ropes. The translation in the first Minnesota edition, following the German exactly, is reprinted here in the passage in double brackets on pages 107–8. E.B.

SHEN TE: No! Don't go, illustrious ones!

FIRST GOD:

> Our cloud has landed now in yonder field
> From which it will transport us back to heaven.
> Farewell, Shen Te, let not thy courage fail
>   thee. . . .

[*Exeunt* GODS.]

SHEN TE: What about the old couple? They've lost their shop? What about the water seller and his hand? And I've got to defend myself against the barber, because I don't love him! And against Sun, because I do love him! How? How? [SHEN TE'S *eyes follow the* GODS *as they are imagined to step into a cloud which rises and moves forward over the orchestra and up beyond the balcony.*]

FIRST GOD [*from on high*]: We have faith in you, Shen Te!

SHEN TE: There'll be a child. And he'll have to be fed. I can't stay here. Where shall I go?

FIRST GOD: Continue to be good, good woman of Setzuan!

SHEN TE: I need my bad cousin!

FIRST GOD: But not very often!

SHEN TE: Once a week at least!

FIRST GOD: Once a month will be quite enough!

SHEN TE [*shrieking*]: No, no! Help!

[*But the cloud continues to recede as the* GODS *sing.*]

VALEDICTORY HYMN

> What rapture, oh, it is to know
>   A good thing when you see it
> And having seen a good thing, oh,
>   What rapture 'tis to flee it
>
> Be good, sweet maid of Setzuan
>   Let Shui Ta be clever
> Departing, we forget the man
>   Remember your endeavour

> Because through all the length of days
> Her goodness faileth never
> Sing hallelujah! Make Shen Te's
> Good name live on forever!

SHEN TE: Help!

*

[[FIRST GOD:
> And now . . . [*He makes a sign and music is heard.*
> *Rosy light.*] let us return.
> This little world has much engaged us.
> Its joy and its sorrow have refreshed and pained
> us.
> Up there, however, beyond the stars,
> We shall gladly think of you, Shen Te, the
> good woman
> Who bears witness to our spirit down below,
> Who, in cold darkness, carries a little lamp!
> Good-bye! Do it well!

[*He makes a sign and the ceiling opens. A pink cloud comes down. On it the* THREE GODS *rise, very slowly.*]

SHEN TE: Oh, don't, illustrious ones! Don't go away! Don't leave me! How can I face the good old couple who've lost their store and the water seller with his stiff hand? And how can I defend myself from the barber whom I do not love and from Sun whom I do love? And I am with child. Soon there'll be a little son who'll want to eat. I can't stay here! [*She turns with a hunted look toward the door which will let her tormentors in.*]

FIRST GOD: You can do it. Just be good and everything will turn out well!

[*Enter the witnesses. They look with surprise at the judges floating on their pink cloud.*]

WONG: Show respect! The gods have appeared among us!

Three of the highest gods have come to Setzuan to find a good human being. They had found one already, but . . .

FIRST GOD: No 'but'! Here she is!

ALL: Shen Te!

FIRST GOD: She has not perished. She was only hidden. She will stay with you. A good human being!

SHEN TE: But I need my cousin!

FIRST GOD: Not too often!

SHEN TE: At least once a week!

FIRST GOD: Once a month. That's enough!

SHEN TE: Oh, don't go away, illustrious ones! I haven't told you everything! I need you desperately!

[*The* GODS *sing.*]

THE TRIO OF THE VANISHING GODS
ON THE CLOUD

Unhappily we cannot stay
More than a fleeting year.
If we watch our find too long
It will disappear.

Here the golden light of truth
With shadow is alloyed
Therefore now we ask your leave
To go back to our void.

SHEN TE: Help! [*Her cries continue through the song.*]

Since our search is over now
Let us fast ascend!
The good woman of Setzuan
Praise we at the end!

[*As* SHEN TE *stretches out her arms to them in desperation, they disappear above, smiling and waving.*]]

Epilogue

You're thinking, aren't you, that this is no right
Conclusion to the play you've seen tonight?
After a tale, exotic, fabulous,
A nasty ending was slipped up on us.
We feel deflated too. We too are nettled
To see the curtain down and nothing settled.
How could a better ending be arranged?
Could one change people? Can the world be changed?
Would new gods do the trick? Will atheism?
Moral rearmament? Materialism?
It is for you to find a way, my friends,
To help good men arrive at happy ends.
You write the happy ending to the play!
There must, there must, there's got to be a way! *

* When I first received the German manuscript of *Good Woman* from Brecht in 1945 it had no Epilogue. He wrote it a little later, influenced by misunderstandings of the ending in the press on the occasion of the Viennese première of the play. I believe that the Epilogue has sometimes been spoken by the actress playing Shen Te, but the actor playing Wong might be a shrewder choice, since the audience has already accepted him as a kind of chorus. On the other hand, it is not *Wong* who should deliver the Epilogue: whichever actor delivers it should drop the character he has been playing. E.B.

The Caucasian Chalk Circle

CHARACTERS

OLD MAN *on the right*
PEASANT WOMAN *on the right*
YOUNG PEASANT
A VERY YOUNG WORKER
OLD MAN *on the left*
PEASANT WOMAN *on the left*
AGRICULTURIST KATO
GIRL TRACTORIST
WOUNDED SOLDIER
THE DELEGATE *from the capital*
THE SINGER
GEORGI ABASHWILI, *the Governor*
NATELLA, *the Governor's wife*
MICHAEL, *their son*
SHALVA, *an adjutant*
ARSEN KAZBEKI, *a fat prince*
MESSENGER *from the capital*
NIKO MIKADZE *and* MIKA LOLADZE, *doctors*
SIMON SHASHAVA, *a soldier*
GRUSHA VASHNADZE, *a kitchen maid*
OLD PEASANT *with the milk*
CORPORAL *and* PRIVATE

PEASANT *and his wife*
LAVRENTI VASHNADZE, *Grusha's brother*
ANIKO, *his wife*
PEASANT WOMAN, *for a while Grusha's mother-in-law*
JUSSUP, *her son*
MONK
AZDAK, *village recorder*
SHAUWA, *a policeman*
GRAND DUKE
DOCTOR
INVALID
LIMPING MAN
BLACKMAILER
LUDOVICA
INNKEEPER, *her father-in-law*
STABLEBOY
POOR OLD PEASANT WOMAN
IRAKLI, *her brother-in-law, a bandit*
THREE WEALTHY FARMERS
ILLO SHUBOLADZE *and* SANDRO OBOLADZE, *lawyers*
OLD MARRIED COUPLE

SOLDIERS, SERVANTS, PEASANTS, BEGGARS,
MUSICIANS, MERCHANTS, NOBLES, ARCHITECTS

NOTE ON THE LOCALE

THE action of the play centres on Nuka (or Nukha), a town in Azerbaijan. However, the 'capital' referred to in the Prologue is not Baku (capital of Azerbaijan) but Tiflis, capital of Georgia. When Azdak, later, refers to 'the capital' he means Nuka itself, though whether Nuka was ever capital of *Georgia* I doubt: in the reading I myself have done on the subject I have only found Nuka to be the capital of a Nuka Khanate. The word 'Georgia' has not been used in this English version, because of its American associations; instead, its alternative name 'Grusinia' (or Gruziya) has been used. The reasons for re-settling the old Chinese story in Transcaucasia are not far to seek. The play was written when the Soviet chief of state, Joseph Stalin, was a Georgian, as was his favourite poet, cited in the Prologue, Mayakovsky. And surely there is a point in having this story acted out at the place where Europe and Asia meet, a place incomparably rich both in legend and history. Here Prometheus was chained to his rock. Here Jason found the Golden Fleece. Here Noah's Ark touched ground. Here the armies of both Genghis Khan and Tamerlane wrought havoc.

E.B.

THE JUDGE: Officer, fetch a piece of chalk. You will trace below the bench a circle, in the centre of which you will place the young child. Then you will order the two women to wait, each of them at opposite sides of the circle. When the real mother takes hold of him, it will be easy for the child to come outside the circle. But the pretended mother cannot lead him out.

[*The* OFFICER *traces a circle with the chalk and motions the* CHILD *to stand in the centre of it.* MRS MA *takes the* CHILD'S *hand and leads him out of the circle.* HAI-TANG *fails to contend with her.*]

THE JUDGE: It is evident that Hai-Tang is not the mother of the child, since she did not come forward to draw him out of the circle.

HAI-TANG: I supplicate you, Honoured Sir, to calm your wrath. If I cannot obtain my son without dislocating his arm or bruising his baby flesh, I would rather perish under the blows than make the least effort to take him out of the circle.

THE JUDGE: A sage of old once said: What man can hide what he really is? Behold the power of the Chalk Circle! In order to seize an inheritance, Mrs Ma has raised a young child that is not her own. But the Chalk Circle augustly brought out the truth and the falsehood. Mrs Ma has an engaging exterior but her heart is corrupt. The true mother – Hai-Tang – is at last recognized.

From *The Chalk Circle*, an anonymous Chinese play of about 1300 A.D.

Prologue

(Summer, 1945)

Among the ruins of a war-ravaged Caucasian village the MEMBERS
*of two Kolkhoz villages, mostly women and older men, are sitting in
a circle, smoking and drinking wine. With them is a* DELEGATE *of
the State Reconstruction Commission from Tifls, the capital.*

PEASANT WOMAN, *left* [*pointing*]: In those hills over there we
stopped three Nazi tanks, but the apple orchard was already
destroyed.

OLD MAN, *right*: Our beautiful dairy farm: a ruin.

GIRL TRACTORIST: I laid the fire, Comrade.

    [*Pause.*]

DELEGATE: I will read the report. 'Delegates from the goat-
breeding Kolkhoz "Rosa Luxemburg" have been to Nuka.
When Hitler's armies approached, this kolkhoz moved its
herds further East, on orders from the authorities. They are
now planning to return. Their delegates have looked over
both the village and the land and found a lot of destruction.
[DELEGATES *on right nod.*] The near-by fruit-culture Kolkhoz
[*to the left*] "Galinsk" proposes to use what used to be Kolkhoz "Rosa Luxemburg's" grazing land for orchards and
vineyards. It's a valley where grass doesn't grow very well.'
As a delegate of the Reconstruction Commission in Nuka,
I request that the two Kolkhoz villages decide between
themselves whether Kolkhoz 'Rosa Luxemburg' can return
here or not.

OLD MAN, *right*: First of all, I want to protest against the time
limit on discussion. We of Kolkhoz 'Rosa Luxemburg' have
spent three days and three nights getting here. And now discussion is limited to half a day.

WOUNDED SOLDIER, *left*: Comrade, we haven't as many villages as we used to have. We haven't as many hands. We haven't as much time.

GIRL TRACTORIST: All pleasures have to be rationed. Tobacco is rationed, and wine. Discussion should be rationed.

OLD MAN, *right* [*sighing*]: Death to the fascists! But I will come to the point and explain why we want our valley back. There are a great many reasons, but I'll begin with one of the simplest. Makinä Abakidze, unpack the goat cheese. [*A* PEASANT WOMAN *from right takes from a basket an enormous cheese wrapped in a cloth. Applause and laughter.*] Help yourselves, Comrades, start in!

OLD MAN, *left* [*suspiciously*]: Is this a way of influencing us?

OLD MAN, *right* [*amid laughter*]: How could it be a way of influencing you, Surab, you valley-thief? Everyone knows you'll take the cheese and the valley, too. [*Laughter.*] All I expect from you is an honest answer. Do you like the cheese?

OLD MAN, *left*: The answer is: yes.

OLD MAN, *right*: Really. [*Bitterly*] I ought to have known you know nothing about cheese.

OLD MAN, *left*: Why not? When I tell you I like it?

OLD MAN, *right*: Because you can't like it. Because it's not what it was in the old days. And why not? Because our goats don't like the new grass as they did the old. Cheese is not cheese because grass is not grass, that's the thing. Please put that in your report.

OLD MAN, *left*: But your cheese is excellent.

OLD MAN, *right*: It isn't excellent. It's just passable. The new grazing land is no good, whatever the young people may say. One can't live there. It doesn't even smell of morning in the morning.

[*Several people laugh.*]

DELEGATE: Don't mind their laughing: they understand you. Comrades, why does one love one's country? Because the bread tastes better there, the air smells better, voices sound stronger, the sky is higher, the ground is easier to walk on. Isn't that so?

OLD MAN, *right*: The valley has belonged to us from all eternity.

SOLDIER, *left*: What does *that* mean – from all eternity? Nothing belongs to anyone from all eternity. When you were young you didn't even belong to yourself. You belonged to the Kazbeki princes.

OLD MAN, *right*: Doesn't it make a difference, though, what kind of trees stand next to the house you are born in? Or what kind of neighbours you have? Doesn't that make a difference? We want to come back just to have you as our neighbours, valley-thieves! Now you can all laugh again.

OLD MAN, *left* [*laughing*]: Then why don't you listen to what your neighbour, Kato Wachtang, our agriculturist, has to say about the valley?

PEASANT WOMAN, *right*: We've not said all we have to say about our valley. By no means. Not all the houses are destroyed. As for the dairy farm, at least the foundation wall is still standing.

DELEGATE: You can claim State support – here and there – you know that. I have suggestions here in my pocket.

PEASANT WOMAN, *right*: Comrade Specialist, we haven't come here to haggle. I can't take your cap and hand you another, and say 'This one's better'. The other one might *be* better, but you *like* yours better.

GIRL TRACTORIST: A piece of land is not a cap – not in our country, Comrade.

DELEGATE: Don't get mad. It's true we have to consider a piece of land as a tool to produce something useful, but it's also true that we must recognize love for a particular piece of land. As far as I'm concerned, I'd like to find out more exactly what you [*to those on the left*] want to do with the valley.

OTHERS: Yes, let Kato speak.

DELEGATE: Comrade Agriculturist!

KATO [*rising; she's in military uniform*]: Comrades, last winter, while we were fighting in these hills here as Partisans, we discussed how, once the Germans were expelled, we could build up our fruit culture to ten times its original size. I've prepared a plan for an irrigation project. By means of a coffer-dam on our mountain lake, 300 hectares of unfertile land can be irrigated. Our Kolkhoz could not only cultivate more fruit, but also have vineyards. The project, however, would only pay if the disputed valley of Kolkhoz 'Rosa Luxemburg' were also included. Here are the calculations. [*She hands* DELEGATE *a briefcase.*]

OLD MAN, *right*: Write into the report that our Kolkhoz plans to start a new stud farm.

GIRL TRACTORIST: Comrades, the project was conceived during days and nights when we had to take cover in the mountains. We were often without ammunition for our half-dozen rifles. Even finding a pencil was difficult. [*Applause from both sides.*]

OLD MAN, *right*: Our thanks to the Comrades of Kolkhoz 'Galinsk' and all those who've defended our country! [*They shake hands and embrace.*]

PEASANT WOMAN, *left*: In doing this our thought was that our soldiers – both your men and our men – should return to a still more productive homeland.

GIRL TRACTORIST: As the poet Mayakovsky said: 'The home of the Soviet people shall also be the home of Reason'!

[*The* DELEGATES *excluding the* OLD MAN *have got up, and with the* DELEGATE *specified proceed to study the Agriculturist's drawings. Exclamations such as:* 'Why is the altitude of fall 22 metres?' – 'This rock must be blown up' – 'Actually, all they need is cement and dynamite' – 'They force water to come down here, that's clever!']

A VERY YOUNG WORKER, *right* [*to* OLD MAN, *right*]: They're going to irrigate all the fields between the hills, look at that, Aleko!

OLD MAN, *right*: I'm not going to look. I knew the project would be good. I won't have a pistol pointed at me!

DELEGATE: But they only want to point a pencil at you!

[*Laughter.*]

OLD MAN, *right* [*gets up gloomily, and walks over to look at the drawings*]: These valley-thieves know only too well that we in this country are suckers for machines and projects.

PEASANT WOMAN, *right*: Aleko Bereshwili, you have a weakness for new projects. That's well known.

DELEGATE: What about my report? May I write that you will all support the cession of your old valley in the interests of this project when you get back to your Kolkhoz?

PEASANT WOMAN, *right*: I will. What about you, Aleko?

OLD MAN, *right* [*bent over drawings*]: I suggest that you give us copies of the drawings to take along.

PEASANT WOMAN, *right*: Then we can sit down and eat. Once he has the drawings and he's ready to discuss them, the matter is settled. I know him. And it will be the same with the rest of us.

[DELEGATES *laughingly embrace again.*]

OLD MAN, *left*: Long live the Kolkhoz 'Rosa Luxemburg' and much luck to your horse-breeding project!

PEASANT WOMAN, *left*: In honour of the visit of the delegates from Kolkhoz 'Rosa Luxemburg' and of the Specialist, the plan is that we all hear a presentation of the Singer Arkadi Tscheidse.

[*Applause.* GIRL TRACTORIST *has gone off to bring the* SINGER.]

PEASANT WOMAN, *right*: Comrades, your entertainment had better be good. It's going to cost us a valley.

PEASANT WOMAN, *left*: Arkadi Tscheidse knows about our discussion. He's promised to perform something that has a bearing on the problem.

KATO: We wired Tiflis three times. The whole thing nearly fell through at the last minute because his driver had a cold.

PEASANT WOMAN, *left*: Arkadi Tscheidse knows 21,000 lines of verse.

OLD MAN, *left*: He's hard to get. You and the Planning Commission should persuade him to come north more often, Comrade.

DELEGATE: We are more interested in economics, I'm afraid.

OLD MAN, *left* [*smiling*]: You arrange the redistribution of vines and tractors, why not songs?

[*Enter the* SINGER *Arkadi Tscheidse, led by* GIRL TRACTORIST. *He is a well-built man of simple manners, accompanied by* FOUR MUSICIANS *with their instruments. The artists are greeted with applause.*]

GIRL TRACTORIST: This is the Comrade Specialist, Arkadi.

[*The* SINGER *greets them all.*]

DELEGATE: Honoured to make your acquaintance. I heard about your songs when I was a boy at school. Will it be one of the old legends?

THE SINGER: A very old one. It's called 'The Chalk Circle' and comes from the Chinese. But we'll do it, of course, in a changed version. Comrades, it's an honour for me to entertain you after a difficult debate. We hope you will find that the voice of the old poet also sounds well in the shadow of Soviet tractors. It may be a mistake to mix different wines, but old and new wisdom mix admirably. Now I hope we'll get something to eat before the performance begins – it would certainly help.

VOICES: Surely. Everyone into the Club House!

[*While everyone begins to move,* DELEGATE *turns to* GIRL TRACTORIST.]

DELEGATE: I hope it won't take long. I've got to get back tonight.

GIRL TRACTORIST: How long will it last, Arkadi? The Comrade Specialist must get back to Tiflis tonight.

THE SINGER [*casually*]: It's actually two stories. A couple of hours.

GIRL TRACTORIST [*confidentially*]: Couldn't you make it shorter?

THE SINGER: No.

VOICE: Arkadi Tscheidse's performance will take place here in the square after the meal.

[*And they all go happily to eat.*]

1. The Noble Child

As the lights go up, the SINGER *is seen sitting on the floor, a black sheepskin cloak round his shoulders, and a little, well-thumbed notebook in his hand. A small group of listeners – the* CHORUS *– sits with him. The manner of his recitation makes it clear that he has told his story over and over again. He mechanically fingers the pages, seldom looking at them. With appropriate gestures, he gives the signal for each scene to begin.*

THE SINGER:
   In olden times, in a bloody time,
   There ruled in a Caucasian city –
   Men called it City of the Damned –
   A Governor.
   His name was Georgi Abashwili.
   He was rich as Croesus
   He had a beautiful wife
   He had a healthy baby.
   No other governor in Grusinia
   Had so many horses in his stable
   So many beggars on his doorstep
   So many soldiers in his service
   So many petitioners in his courtyard.
   Georgi Abashwili – how shall I describe him to you?
   He enjoyed his life.
   On the morning of Easter Sunday
   The Governor and his family went to church.
     [*At the left a large doorway, at the right an even larger gateway.* BEGGARS *and* PETITIONERS *pour from the gateway, holding up thin* CHILDREN, *crutches, and petitions. They are followed by* IRONSHIRTS, *and then, expensively dressed, the* GOVERNOR'S FAMILY.]

BEGGARS AND PETITIONERS: Mercy! Mercy, Your Grace! The taxes are too high.
– I lost my leg in the Persian War, where can I get . . .
– My brother is innocent, Your Grace, a misunderstanding . . .
– The child is starving in my arms!
– Our petition is for our son's discharge from the army, our last remaining son!
– Please, Your Grace, the water inspector takes bribes.
[ONE SERVANT *collects the petitions.* ANOTHER *distributes coins from a purse.* SOLDIERS *push the crowd back, lashing at them with thick leather whips.*]
THE SOLDIER: Get back! Clear the church door!
[*Behind the* GOVERNOR, *his* WIFE, *and the* ADJUTANT, *the* GOVERNOR'S CHILD *is brought through the gateway in an ornate carriage.*]
THE CROWD: The baby!
– I can't see it, don't shove so hard!
– God bless the child, Your Grace!
THE SINGER [*while the crowd is driven back with whips*]:
For the first time on that Easter Sunday, the people saw the Governor's heir.
Two doctors never moved from the noble child, apple of the Governor's eye.
Even the mighty Prince Kazbeki bows before him at the church door.
[*A* FAT PRINCE *steps forward and greets the* FAMILY.]
THE FAT PRINCE: Happy Easter, Natella Abashwili! What a day! When it was raining last night, I thought to myself, gloomy holidays! But this morning the sky was gay. I love a gay sky, a simple heart, Natella Abashwili. And little Michael is a governor from head to foot! Tititi! [*He tickles the* CHILD.]
THE GOVERNOR'S WIFE: What do you think, Arsen, at last Georgi has decided to start building the east wing. All these

wretched slums are to be torn down to make room for the garden.

THE FAT PRINCE: Good news after so much bad! What's the latest on the war, Brother Georgi? [*The* GOVERNOR *indicates a lack of interest.*] Strategical retreat, I hear. Well, minor reverses are to be expected. Sometimes things go well, sometimes not. Such is war. Doesn't mean a thing, does it?

THE GOVERNOR'S WIFE: He's coughing. Georgi, did you hear? [*She speaks sharply to the* DOCTORS, *two dignified men standing close to the little carriage.*] He's coughing!

THE FIRST DOCTOR [*to the* SECOND]: May I remind you, Niko Mikadze, that I was against the lukewarm bath? [*To the* GOVERNOR'S WIFE] There's been a little error over warming the bath water, Your Grace.

THE SECOND DOCTOR [*equally polite*]: Mika Loladze, I'm afraid I can't agree with you. The temperature of the bath water was exactly what our great, beloved Mishiko Oboladze prescribed. More likely a slight draught during the night, Your Grace.

THE GOVERNOR'S WIFE: But do pay more attention to him. He looks feverish, Georgi.

THE FIRST DOCTOR [*bending over the* CHILD]: No cause for alarm, Your Grace. The bath water will be warmer. It won't occur again.

THE SECOND DOCTOR [*with a venomous glance at the* FIRST]: I won't forget that, my dear Mika Loladze. No cause for concern, Your Grace.

THE FAT PRINCE: Well, well, well! I always say: 'A pain in my liver? Then the doctor gets fifty strokes on the soles of his feet.' We live in a decadent age. In the old days one said: 'Off with his head!'

THE GOVERNOR'S WIFE: Let's go into church. Very likely it's the draught here.

[*The procession of* FAMILY *and* SERVANTS *turns into the doorway. The* FAT PRINCE *follows, but the* GOVERNOR *is kept back by the* ADJUTANT, *a handsome young man. When the crowd of* PETITIONERS *has been driven off, a young dust-stained* RIDER, *his arm in a sling, remains behind.*]

THE ADJUTANT [*pointing at the* RIDER, *who steps forward*]: Won't you hear the messenger from the capital, Your Excellency? He arrived this morning. With confidential papers.

THE GOVERNOR: Not before Service, Shalva. But did you hear Brother Kazbeki wish me a happy Easter? Which is all very well, but I don't believe it did rain last night.

THE ADJUTANT [*nodding*]: We must investigate.

THE GOVERNOR: Yes, at once. Tomorrow.

[*They pass through the doorway. The* RIDER, *who has waited in vain for an audience, turns sharply round and, muttering a curse, goes off. Only one of the palace guards –* SIMON SHA-SHAVA *– remains at the door.*]

THE SINGER:

The city is still.

Pigeons strut in the church square.

A soldier of the Palace Guard

Is joking with a kitchen maid

As she comes up from the river with a bundle.

[*A girl –* GRUSHA VASHNADZE *– comes through the gateway with a bundle made of large green leaves under her arm.*]

SIMON: What, the young lady is not in church? Shirking?

GRUSHA: I was dressed to go. But they needed another goose for the banquet. And they asked me to get it. I know about geese.

SIMON: A goose? [*He feigns suspicion.*] I'd like to see that goose. [GRUSHA *does not understand.*] One must be on one's guard with women. 'I only went for a fish,' they tell you, but it turns out to be something else.

GRUSHA [*walking resolutely toward him and showing him the goose*]: There! If it isn't a fifteen-pound goose stuffed full of corn, I'll eat the feathers.

SIMON: A queen of a goose! The Governor himself will eat it. So the young lady has been down to the river again?

GRUSHA: Yes, at the poultry farm.

SIMON: Really? At the poultry farm, down by the river ... not higher up maybe? Near those willows?

GRUSHA: I only go to the willows to wash the linen.

SIMON [insinuatingly]: Exactly.

GRUSHA. Exactly what?

SIMON [winking]: Exactly that.

GRUSHA: Why shouldn't I wash the linen by the willows?

SIMON [with exaggerated laughter]: 'Why shouldn't I wash the linen by the willows!' That's good, really good!

GRUSHA: I don't understand the soldier. What's so good about it?

SIMON [slyly]: 'If something I know someone learns, she'll grow hot and cold by turns!'

GRUSHA: I don't know what I could learn about those willows.

SIMON: Not even if there was a bush opposite? That one could see everything from? Everything that goes on there when a certain person is – 'washing linen'?

GRUSHA: What does go on? Won't the soldier say what he means and have done?

SIMON: Something goes on. Something can be seen.

GRUSHA: Could the soldier mean I dip my toes in the water when it's hot? There's nothing else.

SIMON: There's more. Your toes. And more.

GRUSHA: More what? At most my foot?

SIMON: Your foot. And a little more. [He laughs heartily.]

GRUSHA [angrily]: Simon Shashava, you ought to be ashamed of yourself! To sit in a bush on a hot day and wait till a girl comes and dips her legs in the river! And I bet you bring a friend along too! [She runs off.]

SIMON [shouting after her]: I didn't bring any friend along!

[As the SINGER resumes his tale, the SOLDIER steps into the doorway as though to listen to the service.]

THE SINGER:
The city lies still
But why are there armed men?
The Governor's palace is at peace
But why is it a fortress?
And the Governor returned to his palace
And the fortress was a trap
And the goose was plucked and roasted
But the goose was not eaten this time
And noon was no longer the hour to eat:
Noon was the hour to die.

[*From the doorway at the left the* FAT PRINCE *quickly appears, stands still, looks around. Before the gateway at the right* TWO IRONSHIRTS *are squatting and playing dice. The* FAT PRINCE *sees them, walks slowly past, making a sign to them. They rise: one goes through the gateway, the other goes off at the right. Muffled voices are heard from various directions in the rear:* 'To your posts!' *The palace is surrounded. The* FAT PRINCE *quickly goes off. Church bells in the distance. Enter, through the doorway, the* GOVERNOR'S FAMILY *and procession, returning from church.*]

THE GOVERNOR'S WIFE [*passing the* ADJUTANT]: It's impossible to live in such a slum. But Georgi, of course, will only build for his little Michael. Never for me! Michael is all! All for Michael!

[*The procession turns into the gateway. Again the* ADJUTANT *lingers behind. He waits. Enter the wounded* RIDER *from the doorway.* TWO IRONSHIRTS *of the Palace Guard have taken up positions by the gateway.*]

THE ADJUTANT [*to the* RIDER]: The Governor does not wish to receive military news before dinner – especially if it's depressing, as I assume. In the afternoon His Excellency will confer with prominent architects. They're coming to dinner too. And here they are! [*Enter* THREE GENTLEMEN *through the doorway.*] Go to the kitchen and eat, my friend. [*As the*

RIDER *goes, the* ADJUTANT *greets the* ARCHITECTS.] Gentlemen, His Excellency expects you at dinner. He will devote all his time to you and your great new plans. Come!

ONE OF THE ARCHITECTS: We marvel that His Excellency intends to build. There are disquieting rumours that the war in Persia has taken a turn for the worse.

THE ADJUTANT. All the more reason to build! There's nothing to those rumours anyway. Persia is a long way off, and the garrison here would let itself be hacked to bits for its Governor. [*Noise from the palace. The shrill scream of a woman. Someone is shouting orders. Dumbfounded, the* ADJUTANT *moves toward the gateway. An* IRONSHIRT *steps out, points his lance at him.*] What's this? Put down that lance, you dog.

ONE OF THE ARCHITECTS: It's the Princes! Don't you know the Princes met last night in the capital? And they're against the Grand Duke and his Governors? Gentlemen, we'd better make ourselves scarce. [*They rush off.*]

[*The* ADJUTANT *remains helplessly behind.*]

THE ADJUTANT [*furiously to the Palace Guard*]: Down with those lances! Don't you see the Governor's life is threatened?

[*The* IRONSHIRTS *of the Palace Guard refuse to obey. They stare coldly and indifferently at the* ADJUTANT *and follow the next events without interest.*]

THE SINGER.
O blindness of the great!
They go their way like gods,
Great over bent backs,
Sure of hired fists,
Trusting in the power
Which has lasted so long.
But long is not forever.
O change from age to age!
Thou hope of the people!

[*Enter the* GOVERNOR, *through the gateway, between* TWO

SOLDIERS *armed to the teeth. He is in chains. His face is grey.*]

Up, great sir, deign to walk upright!

From your palace the eyes of many foes follow you!

And now you don't need an architect, a carpenter will do.

You won't be moving into a new palace

But into a little hole in the ground.

Look about you once more, blind man!

   [*The* ARRESTED MAN *looks round.*]

Does all you had please you?

Between the Easter Mass and the Easter meal

You are walking to a place whence no one returns.

   [*The* GOVERNOR *is led off. A horn sounds an alarm. Noise behind the gateway.*]

When the house of a great one collapses

Many little ones are slain.

Those who had no share in the *good* fortunes of the
     mighty

Often have a share in their *mis*fortunes.

The plunging wagon

Drags the sweating oxen down with it

Into the abyss.

   [*The* SERVANTS *come rushing through the gateway in panic.*]

THE SERVANTS [*among themselves*]: The baskets!

– Take them all into the third courtyard! Food for five days!

– The mistress has fainted! Someone must carry her down.

– She must get away.

– What about us? We'll be slaughtered like chickens, as always.

– Goodness, what'll happen? There's bloodshed already in the city, they say.

– Nonsense, the Governor has just been asked to appear at a Princes' meeting. All very correct. Everything'll be ironed out. I heard this on the best authority . . .

[*The* TWO DOCTORS *rush into the courtyard.*]

THE FIRST DOCTOR [*trying to restrain the other*]: Niko Mikadze, it is your duty as a doctor to attend Natella Abashwili.

THE SECOND DOCTOR: My duty! It's yours!

THE FIRST DOCTOR: Whose turn is it to look after the child today, Niko Mikadze, yours or mine?

THE SECOND DOCTOR: Do you really think, Mika Loladze, I'm going to stay a minute longer in this accursed house on that little brat's account? [*They start fighting. All one hears is:* 'You neglect your duty!' *and* 'Duty, my foot!' *Then the* SECOND DOCTOR *knocks the* FIRST *down.*] Go to hell! [*Exit.*]

[*Enter the soldier,* SIMON SHASHAVA. *He searches in the crowd for* GRUSHA.]

SIMON: Grusha! There you are at last! What are you going to do?

GRUSHA: Nothing. If worst comes to worst, I've a brother in the mountains. How about you?

SIMON: Forget about me. [*Formally again*] Grusha Vashnadze, your wish to know my plans fills me with satisfaction. I've been ordered to accompany Madam Natella Abashwili as her guard.

GRUSHA: But hasn't the Palace Guard mutinied?

SIMON [*seriously*]: That's a fact.

GRUSHA: Isn't it dangerous to go with her?

SIMON: In Tiflis, they say: Isn't the stabbing dangerous for the knife?

GRUSHA: You're not a knife, you're a man, Simon Shashava, what has that woman to do with you?

SIMON: That woman has nothing to do with me. I have my orders, and I go.

GRUSHA: The soldier is pigheaded: he is running into danger for nothing – nothing at all. I must get into the third courtyard, I'm in a hurry.

SIMON: Since we're both in a hurry we shouldn't quarrel. You need time for a good quarrel. May I ask if the young lady still has parents?

GRUSHA: No, just a brother.

SIMON: As time is short – my second question is this: Is the young lady as healthy as a fish in water?

GRUSHA: I may have a pain in the right shoulder once in a while. Otherwise I'm strong enough for my job. No one has complained. So far.

SIMON: That's well known. When it's Easter Sunday, and the question arises who'll run for the goose all the same, she'll be the one. My third question is this: Is the young lady impatient? Does she want apples in winter?

GRUSHA: Impatient? No. But if a man goes to war without any reason and then no message comes – that's bad.

SIMON: A message will come. And now my final question ...

GRUSHA: Simon Shashava, I must get to the third courtyard at once. My answer is yes.

SIMON [*very embarrassed*]: Haste, they say, is the wind that blows down the scaffolding. But they also say: The rich don't know what haste is. I'm from ...

GRUSHA: Kutsk ...

SIMON: The young lady has been inquiring about me? I'm healthy, I have no dependants, I make ten piastres a month, as paymaster twenty piastres, and I'm asking – very sincerely – for your hand.

GRUSHA: Simon Shashava, it suits me well.

SIMON [*taking from his neck a thin chain with a little cross on it*]: My mother gave me this cross, Grusha Vashnadze. The chain is silver. Please wear it.

GRUSHA: Many thanks, Simon.

SIMON [*hangs it round her neck*]: It would be better to go to the third courtyard now. Or there'll be difficulties. Anyway, I must harness the horses. The young lady will understand?

GRUSHA: Yes, Simon.

[*They stand undecided.*]

SIMON: I'll just take the mistress to the troops that have stayed loyal. When the war's over, I'll be back. In two weeks. Or three. I hope my intended won't get tired, awaiting my return.

GRUSHA:
>Simon Shashava, I shall wait for you.
>Go calmly into battle, soldier
>The bloody battle, the bitter battle
>From which not everyone returns:
>When you return I shall be there.
>I shall be waiting for you under the green elm
>I shall be waiting for you under the bare elm
>I shall wait until the last soldier has returned
>And longer.
>When you come back from the battle
>No boots will stand at my door
>The pillow beside mine will be empty
>And my mouth will be unkissed.
>When you return, when you return
>You will be able to say: It is just as it was.

SIMON: I thank you, Grusha Vashnadze. And good-bye! [*He bows low before her. She does the same before him. Then she runs quickly off without looking round.*]

[*Enter the* ADJUTANT *from the gateway.*]

THE ADJUTANT [*harshly*]: Harness the horses to the carriage! Don't stand there doing nothing, louse!

[SIMON SHASHAVA *stands to attention and goes off.* TWO SERVANTS *crowd from the gateway, bent low under huge trunks. Behind them, supported by her* WOMEN, *stumbles* NATELLA ABASHWILI. *She is followed by a* WOMAN *carrying the* CHILD.]

THE GOVERNOR'S WIFE: I hardly know if my head's still on. Where's Michael? Don't hold him so clumsily. Pile the trunks onto the carriage. No news from the city, Shalva?

THE ADJUTANT: None. All's quiet so far, but there's not a

minute to lose. No room for all these trunks in the carriage. Pick out what you need. [*Exit quickly.*]

THE GOVERNOR'S WIFE: Only essentials! Quick, open the trunks! I'll tell you what I need. [*The trunks are lowered and opened. She points at some brocade dresses.*] The green one! And, of course, the one with the fur trimming. Where are Niko Mikadze and Mika Loladze? I've suddenly got the most terrible migraine again. It always starts in the temples. [*Enter* GRUSHA.] Taking your time, eh? Go and get the hot water bottles this minute! [GRUSHA *runs off, returns later with hot water bottles; the* GOVERNOR'S WIFE *orders her about by signs.*] Don't tear the sleeves.

A YOUNG WOMAN: Pardon, madam, no harm has come to the dress.

THE GOVERNOR'S WIFE: Because I stopped you. I've been watching you for a long time. Nothing in your head but making eyes at Shalva Tzereteli. I'll kill you, you bitch! [*She beats the* YOUNG WOMAN.]

THE ADJUTANT [*appearing in the gateway*]: Please make haste, Natella Abashwili. Firing has broken out in the city. [*Exit.*]

THE GOVERNOR'S WIFE [*letting go of the* YOUNG WOMAN]: Oh dear, do you think they'll lay hands on us? Why should they? Why? [*She herself begins to rummage in the trunks.*] How's Michael? Asleep?

THE WOMAN WITH THE CHILD: Yes, madam.

THE GOVERNOR'S WIFE: Then put him down a moment and get my little saffron-coloured boots from the bedroom. I need them for the green dress. [*The* WOMAN *puts down the* CHILD *and goes off.*] Just look how these things have been packed! No love! No understanding! If you don't give them every order yourself . . . At such moments you realize what kind of servants you have! They gorge themselves at your expense, and never a word of gratitude! I'll remember this.

THE ADJUTANT [*entering, very excited*]: Natella, you must leave at once!

THE GOVERNOR'S WIFE: Why? I've got to take this silver dress – it cost a thousand piastres. And that one there, and where's the wine-coloured one?

THE ADJUTANT [*trying to pull her away*]: Riots have broken out! We must leave at once. Where's the baby?

THE GOVERNOR'S WIFE [*calling to the* YOUNG WOMAN *who was holding the baby*]: Maro, get the baby ready! Where on earth are you?

THE ADJUTANT [*leaving*]: We'll probably have to leave the carriage behind and go ahead on horseback.

[*The* GOVERNOR'S WIFE *rummages again among her dresses, throws some onto the heap of chosen clothes, then takes them off again. Noises, drums are heard. The* YOUNG WOMAN *who was beaten creeps away. The sky begins to grow red.*]

THE GOVERNOR'S WIFE [*rummaging desperately*]: I simply cannot find the wine-coloured dress. Take the whole pile to the carriage. Where's Asja? And why hasn't Maro come back? Have you all gone crazy?

THE ADJUTANT [*returning*]: Quick! Quick!

THE GOVERNOR'S WIFE [*to the* FIRST WOMAN]: Run! Just throw them into the carriage!

THE ADJUTANT: We're not taking the carriage. And if you don't come now, I'll ride off on my own.

THE GOVERNOR'S WIFE [*as the* FIRST WOMAN *can't carry everything*]: Where's that bitch Asja? [*The* ADJUTANT *pulls her away.*] Maro, bring theba by! [*To the* FIRST WOMAN] Go and look for Masha. No, first take the dresses to the carriage. Such nonsense! I wouldn't dream of going on horseback! [*Turning round, she sees the red sky, and starts back rigid. The fire burns. She is pulled out by the* ADJUTANT. *Shaking, the* FIRST WOMAN *follows with the dresses.*]

MARO [*from the doorway with the boots*]: Madam! [*She sees the trunks and dresses and runs toward the* BABY, *picks it up, and holds it a moment.*] They left it behind, the beasts. [*She hands it to* GRUSHA.] Hold it a moment. [*She runs off, following the* GOVERNOR'S WIFE.]

[*Enter* SERVANTS *from the gateway.*]

THE COOK: Well, so they've actually gone. Without the food wagons, and not a minute too early. It's time for us to clear out.

A GROOM: This'll be an unhealthy neighbourhood for quite a while. [*To* ONE OF THE WOMEN] Suliko, take a few blankets and wait for me in the foal stables.

GRUSHA: What have they done with the Governor?

THE GROOM [*gesturing throat cutting*]: Ffffft.

A FAT WOMAN [*seeing the gesture and becoming hysterical*]: Oh dear, oh dear, oh dear, oh dear! Our master Georgi Abashwili! A picture of health he was, at the morning Mass – and now! Oh, take me away, we're all lost, we must die in sin like our master, Georgi Abashwili!

THE OTHER WOMAN [*soothing her*]: Calm down, Nina! You'll be taken to safety. You've never hurt a fly.

THE FAT WOMAN [*being led out*]: Oh dear, oh dear, oh dear! Quick! Let's all get out before they come, before they come!

A YOUNG WOMAN: Nina takes it more to heart than the mistress, that's a fact. They even have to have their weeping done for them.

THE COOK: We'd better get out, all of us.

ANOTHER WOMAN [*glancing back*]: That must be the East Gate burning.

THE YOUNG WOMAN [*seeing the* CHILD *in* GRUSHA'S *arms*]: The baby! What are you doing with it?

GRUSHA: It got left behind.

THE YOUNG WOMAN: She simply left it there. Michael, who was kept out of all the draughts!

[*The* SERVANTS *gather round the* CHILD.]

GRUSHA: He's waking up.

THE GROOM: Better put him down, I tell you. I'd rather not think what'd happen to anybody who was found with that baby.

THE COOK: That's right. Once they get started, they'll kill each other off, whole families at a time. Let's go.

[*Exeunt all but* GRUSHA, *with the* CHILD *on her arm, and* TWO WOMEN.]

THE TWO WOMEN: Didn't you hear? Better put him down.

GRUSHA: The nurse asked me to hold him a moment.

THE OLDER WOMAN: She's not coming back, you simpleton.

THE YOUNGER WOMAN: Keep your hands off it.

THE OLDER WOMAN [*amiably*]: Grusha, you're a good soul, but you're not very bright, and you know it. I tell you, if he had the plague he couldn't be more dangerous.

GRUSHA [*stubbornly*]: He hasn't got the plague. He looks at me! He's human!

THE OLDER WOMAN: Don't look at *him*. You're a fool – the kind that always get put upon. A person need only say, 'Run for the salad, you have the longest legs', and you run. My husband has an ox cart – you can come with us if you hurry! Lord, by now the whole neighbourhood must be in flames.

[BOTH WOMEN *leave, sighing. After some hesitation,* GRUSHA *puts the sleeping* CHILD *down, looks at it for a moment, then takes a brocade blanket from the heap of clothes and covers it. Then* BOTH WOMEN *return, dragging bundles.* GRUSHA *starts guiltily away from the* CHILD *and walks a few steps to one side.*]

THE YOUNGER WOMAN: Haven't you packed anything yet? There isn't much time, you know. The Ironshirts will be here from the barracks.

GRUSHA: Coming! [*She runs through the doorway.*]

[BOTH WOMEN *go to the gateway and wait. The sound of horses is heard. They flee, screaming. Enter the* FAT PRINCE *with drunken* IRONSHIRTS. *One of them carries the Governor's head on a lance.*]

THE FAT PRINCE: Here! In the middle! [ONE SOLDIER *climbs onto the* OTHER'S *back, takes the head, holds it tentatively over the door.*] That's not the middle. Farther to the right. That's it. What I do, my friends, I do well. [*While, with hammer and nail, the* SOLDIER *fastens the head to the wall by its hair*] This morning at the church door I said to Georgi Abashwili: 'I love a clear sky.' Actually, I prefer the lightning that comes out of a clear sky. Yes, indeed. It's a pity they took the brat along, though, I need him, urgently. [*Exit with* IRONSHIRTS *through the gateway.*]

> [*Trampling of horses again. Enter* GRUSHA *through the door-way looking cautiously about her. Clearly she has waited for the* IRONSHIRTS *to go. Carrying a bundle, she walks to-ward the gateway. At the last moment, she turns to see if the* CHILD *is still there. Catching sight of the head over the door-way, she screams. Horrified, she picks up her bundle again, and is about to leave when the* SINGER *starts to speak. She stands rooted to the spot.*]

THE SINGER:

As she was standing between courtyard and gate,
She heard or she thought she heard a low voice calling.
The child called to her,
Not whining, but calling quite sensibly,
Or so it seemed to her.
'Woman,' it said, 'help me.'
And it went on, not whining, but saying quite sensibly:
'Know, woman, he who hears not a cry for help
But passes by with troubled ears will never hear
The gentle call of a lover nor the blackbird at dawn
Nor the happy sigh of the tired grape-picker as the
     Angelus rings.'
[*She walks a few steps toward the* CHILD *and bends over it.*]
Hearing this she went back for one more look at the child:
Only to sit with him for a moment or two,
Only till someone should come,
His mother, or anyone.
[*Leaning on a trunk, she sits facing the* CHILD.]

Only till she would have to leave, for the danger was too
 great,
The city was full of flame and crying.
   [*The light grows dimmer, as though evening and night were
   coming on.*]
Fearful is the seductive power of goodness!
   [GRUSHA *now settles down to watch over the* CHILD *through
   the night. Once, she lights a small lamp to look at it. Once, she
   tucks it in with a coat. From time to time she listens and looks to
   see whether someone is coming.*]
And she sat with the child a long time,
Till evening came, till night came, till dawn came.
She sat too long, too long she saw
The soft breathing, the small clenched fists,
Till toward morning the seduction was complete
And she rose, and bent down and, sighing, took the child
And carried it away.
   [*She does what the* SINGER *says as he describes it.*]
As if it was stolen goods she picked it up.
As if she was a thief she crept away.

2. The Flight into the Northern Mountains

THE SINGER:
   When Grusha Vashnadze left the city
   On the Grusinian highway
   On the way to the Northern Mountains
   She sang a song, she bought some milk.
THE CHORUS:
   How will this human child escape
   The bloodhounds, the trap-setters?
   Into the deserted mountains she journeyed
   Along the Grusinian highway she journeyed
   She sang a song, she bought some milk.

[GRUSHA VASHNADZE *walks on. On her back she carries the* CHILD *in a sack, in one hand is a large stick, in the other a bundle. She sings.*]

THE SONG OF THE FOUR GENERALS

Four generals
Set out for Iran.
With the first one, war did not agree.
The second never won a victory.
For the third the weather was never right.
For the fourth the men would never fight.
Four generals
And not a single man!

Sosso Robakidse
Went marching to Iran
With him the war did so agree
He soon had won a victory.
For him the weather was always right.
For him the men would always fight.
Sosso Robakidse,
He is our man!

[*A peasant's cottage appears.*]

GRUSHA [*to the* CHILD]: Noontime is meal time. Now we'll sit hopefully in the grass, while the good Grusha goes and buys a little pitcher of milk. [*She lays the* CHILD *down and knocks at the cottage door. An* OLD MAN *opens it.*] Grandfather, could I have a little pitcher of milk? And a corn cake, maybe?

THE OLD MAN: Milk? We have no milk. The soldiers from the city have our goats. Go to the soldiers if you want milk.

GRUSHA: But grandfather, you must have a little pitcher of milk for a baby?

THE OLD MAN. And for a God-bless-you, eh?

GRUSHA: Who said anything about a God-bless-you? [*She shows her purse.*] We'll pay like princes. 'Head in the clouds, backside in the water.' [*The* PEASANT *goes off, grumbling, for milk.*] How much for the milk?

THE OLD MAN: Three piastres. Milk has gone up.

GRUSHA: Three piastres for this little drop? [*Without a word the* OLD MAN *shuts the door in her face.*] Michael, did you hear that? Three piastres! We can't afford it! [*She goes back, sits down again, and gives the* CHILD *her breast.*] Suck. Think of the three piastres. There's nothing there, but you *think* you're drinking, and that's something. [*Shaking her head, she sees that the* CHILD *isn't sucking any more. She gets up, walks back to the door, and knocks again.*] Open, grandfather, we'll pay. [*Softly*] May lightning strike you! [*When the* OLD MAN *appears*] I thought it would be half a piastre. But the baby must be fed. How about one piastre for that little drop?

THE OLD MAN: Two.

GRUSHA: Don't shut the door again. [*She fishes a long time in her bag.*] Here are two piastres. The milk better be good. I still have two days' journey ahead of me. It's a murderous business you have here – and sinful, too!

THE OLD MAN: Kill the soldiers if you want milk.

GRUSHA [*giving the* CHILD *some milk*]: This is an expensive joke. Take a sip, Michael, it's a week's pay. Around here they think we earned our money just sitting around. Oh, Michael, Michael, you're a nice little load for a girl to take on! [*Uneasy, she gets up, puts the* CHILD *on her back, and walks on.*]

[*The* OLD MAN, *grumbling, picks up the pitcher and looks after her unmoved.*]

THE SINGER:

As Grusha Vashnadze went northward
The Princes' Ironshirts went after her.

THE CHORUS:

How will the barefoot girl escape the Ironshirts,

The bloodhounds, the trap-setters?
They hunt even by night.
Pursuers never tire.
Butchers sleep little.

[TWO IRONSHIRTS *are trudging along the highway*.]

THE CORPORAL: You'll never amount to anything, block-head, your heart's not in it. Your senior officer sees this in little things. Yesterday, when I made the fat gal, yes, you grabbed her husband as I commanded, and you did kick him in the belly, at my request, but did you *enjoy* it, like a loyal Private, or were you just doing your duty? I've kept an eye on you blockhead, you're a hollow reed and a tink-ling cymbal, you won't get promoted. [*They walk a while in silence*.] Don't think I've forgotten how insubordinate you are, either. Stop limping! I forbid you to limp! You limp because I sold the horses, and I sold the horses because I'd never have got that price again. You limp to show me you don't like marching. I know you. It won't help. You wait. Sing!

THE TWO IRONSHIRTS [*singing*]:
Sadly to war I went my way
Leaving my loved one at her door.
My friends will keep her honour safe
Till from the war I'm back once more.

THE CORPORAL: Louder!

THE TWO IRONSHIRTS [*singing*]:
When 'neath a headstone I shall be
My love a little earth will bring:
'Here rest the feet that oft would run to me
And here the arms that oft to me would cling.'

[*They begin to walk again in silence*.]

THE CORPORAL: A good soldier has his heart and soul in it. When he receives an order, he gets a hard on, and when he drives his lance into the enemy's guts, he comes. [*He shouts for joy*.] He lets himself be torn to bits for his superior officer, and as he lies dying he takes note that his corporal is nodding approval, and that is reward enough, it's his dearest wish. You won't get any nod of approval, but you'll croak all right. Christ, how'm I to get my hands on the Governor's bastard with the help of a fool like you! [*They stay on stage behind.*]

THE SINGER:

When Grusha Vashnadze came to the River Sirra

Flight grew too much for her, the helpless child too heavy.

In the cornfields the rosy dawn

Is cold to the sleepless one, only cold.

The gay clatter of the milk cans in the farmyard where the smoke rises

Is only a threat to the fugitive.

She who carries the child feels its weight and little more.

[GRUSHA *stops in front of a farm. A fat* PEASANT WOMAN *is carrying a milk can through the door.* GRUSHA *waits until she has gone in, then approaches the house cautiously.*]

GRUSHA [*to the* CHILD]: Now you've wet yourself again, and you know I've no linen. Michael, this is where we part company. It's far enough from the city. They wouldn't want you *so* much that they'd follow you all *this* way, little good-for-nothing. The peasant woman is kind, and can't you just smell the milk? [*She bends down to lay the* CHILD *on the threshold.*] So farewell, Michael, I'll forget how you kicked me in the back all night to make me walk faster. And you can forget the meagre fare – it was meant well. I'd like to have kept you – your nose is so tiny – but it can't be. I'd have shown you your first rabbit, I'd have trained you to keep dry, but now I must turn around. My sweetheart the soldier might be back soon, and suppose he didn't find me? You can't ask that, can you?

[*She creeps up to the door and lays the* CHILD *on the threshold. Then, hiding behind a tree, she waits until the* PEASANT WOMAN *opens the door and sees the bundle.*]

THE PEASANT WOMAN: Good heavens, what's this? Husband!

THE PEASANT: What is it? Let me finish my soup.

THE PEASANT WOMAN [*to the* CHILD]: Where's your mother then? Haven't you got one? It's a boy. Fine linen. He's from a good family, you can see that. And they just leave him on our doorstep. Oh, these are times!

THE PEASANT: If they think we're going to feed it, they're wrong. You can take it to the priest in the village. That's the best we can do.

THE PEASANT WOMAN: What'll the priest do with him? He needs a mother. There, he's waking up. Don't you think we could keep him, though?

THE PEASANT [*shouting*]: No!

THE PEASANT WOMAN: I could lay him in the corner by the armchair. All I need is a crib. I can take him into the fields with me. See him laughing? Husband, we have a roof over our heads. We can do it. Not another word out of you! [*She carries the* CHILD *into the house.*]

[*The* PEASANT *follows protesting.* GRUSHA *steps out from behind the tree, laughs, and hurries off in the opposite direction.*]

THE SINGER:
Why so cheerful, making for home?

THE CHORUS:
Because the child has won new parents with a laugh,
Because I'm rid of the little one, I'm cheerful.

THE SINGER:
And why so sad?

THE CHORUS:
Because I'm single and free, I'm sad
Like someone who's been robbed
Someone who's newly poor.

[*She walks for a short while, then meets the the* TWO IRON-SHIRTS *who point their lances at her.*]

THE CORPORAL: Lady, you are running straight into the arms of the Armed Forces. Where are you coming from? And when? Are you having illicit relations with the enemy? Where is he hiding? What movements is he making in your rear? How about the hills? How about the valleys? How are your stockings held in position? [GRUSHA *stands there frightened.*] Don't be scared, we always withdraw, if necessary ... what, blockhead? I always withdraw. In that respect at least, I can be relied on. Why are you staring like that at my lance? In the field no soldier drops his lance, that's a rule. Learn it by heart, blockhead. Now lady, where are you headed?

GRUSHA: To meet my intended, one Simon Shashava, of the Palace Guard in Nuka.

THE CORPORAL: Simon Shashava? Sure, I know him. He gave me the key so I could look you up once in a while. Blockhead, we are getting to be unpopular. We must make her realize we have honourable intentions. Lady, behind apparent frivolity I conceal a serious nature, so let me tell you officially: I want a child from you. [GRUSHA *utters a little scream.*] Blockhead, she understood me. Uh-huh, isn't it a sweet shock? 'Then first I must take the noodles out of the oven, Officer. Then first I must change my torn shirt, Colonel.' But away with jokes, away with my lance! We are looking for a baby. A baby from a good family. Have you heard of such a baby, from the city, dressed in fine linen, and suddenly turning up here?

GRUSHA: No, I haven't heard a thing. [*Suddenly she turns round and runs back panic-stricken.*]

[*The* IRONSHIRTS *glance at each other, then follow her, cursing.*]

THE SINGER:
Run, kind girl! The killers are coming!
Help the helpless babe, helpless girl!
And so she runs!

THE CHORUS:
In the bloodiest times

There are kind people.

[*As* GRUSHA *rushes into the cottage, the* PEASANT WOMAN *is bending over the* CHILD'S *crib.*]

GRUSHA: Hide him. Quick! The Ironshirts are coming! I laid him on your doorstep. But he isn't mine. He's from a good family.

THE PEASANT WOMAN: Who's coming? What Ironshirts?

GRUSHA Don't ask questions. The Ironshirts that are looking for it.

THE PEASANT WOMAN: They've no business in my house. But I must have a little talk with you, it seems.

GRUSHA: Take off the fine linen. It'll give us away.

THE PEASANT WOMAN: Linen, my foot! In this house I make the decisions! 'You can't vomit in *my* room!' Why did you abandon it? It's a sin.

GRUSHA [*looking out of the window*]: Look, they're coming out from behind those trees! I shouldn't have run away, it made them angry. Oh, what shall I do?

THE PEASANT WOMAN [*looking out of the window and suddenly starting with fear*]: Gracious! Ironshirts!

GRUSHA: They're after the baby.

THE PEASANT WOMAN: Suppose they come in!

GRUSHA: You mustn't give him to them. Say he's yours.

THE PEASANT WOMAN: Yes.

GRUSHA: They'll run him through if you hand him over.

THE PEASANT WOMAN: But suppose they ask for it? The silver for the harvest is in the house.

GRUSHA: If you let them have him, they'll run him through, right here in this room! You've got to say he's yours!

THE PEASANT WOMAN: Yes. But what if they don't believe me?

GRUSHA: You must be firm.

THE PEASANT WOMAN: They'll burn the roof over our heads.

GRUSHA: That's why you must say he's yours. His name's Michael. But I shouldn't have told you. [*The* PEASANT

WOMAN *nods*.] Don't nod like that. And don't tremble – they'll notice.

THE PEASANT WOMAN: Yes.

GRUSHA: And stop saying yes, I can't stand it. [*She shakes the* WOMAN] Don't you have any children?

THE PEASANT WOMAN [*muttering*]: He's in the war.

GRUSHA: Then maybe *he's* an Ironshirt? Do you want *him* to run children through with a lance? You'd bawl him out. 'No fooling with lances in my house!' you'd shout, 'is that what I've reared you for? Wash your neck before you speak to your mother!'

THE PEASANT WOMAN: That's true, he couldn't get away with anything around here!

GRUSHA: So you'll say he's yours?

THE PEASANT WOMAN: Yes.

GRUSHA: Look! They're coming!

[*There is a knocking at the door. The* WOMEN *don't answer. Enter* IRONSHIRTS. *The* PEASANT WOMAN *bows low*.]

THE CORPORAL: Well, here she is. What did I tell you? What a nose I have! I *smelt* her. Lady, I have a question for you. Why did you run away? What did you think I would do to you? I'll bet it was something dirty. Confess!

GRUSHA [*while the* PEASANT WOMAN *bows again and again*]: I'd left some milk on the stove, and I suddenly remembered it.

THE CORPORAL: Or maybe you imagined I looked at you in a dirty way? Like there could be something between us? A lewd sort of look, know what I mean?

GRUSHA: I didn't see it.

THE CORPORAL: But it's possible, huh? You admit that much. After all, I might be a pig. I'll be frank with you: I could think of all sorts of things if we were alone. [*To the* PEASANT WOMAN] Shouldn't you be busy in the yard? Feeding the hens?

THE PEASANT WOMAN [*falling suddenly to her knees*]: Soldier,

I didn't know a thing about it. Please don't burn the roof over our heads.

THE CORPORAL: What are you talking about?

THE PEASANT WOMAN: I had nothing to do with it. She left it on my doorstep, I swear it!

THE CORPORAL [*suddenly seeing the* CHILD *and whistling*]: Ah, so there's a little something in the crib! Blockhead, I smell a thousand piastres. Take the old girl outside and hold on to her. It looks like I have a little cross-examining to do. [*The* PEASANT WOMAN *lets herself be led out by the* PRIVATE, *without a word.*] So, you've got the child I wanted from you! [*He walks toward the crib.*]

GRUSHA: Officer, he's mine. He's not the one you're after.

THE CORPORAL: I'll just take a look. [*He bends over the crib.* GRUSHA *looks round in despair.*]

GRUSHA: He's mine! He's mine!

THE CORPORAL: Fine linen!

[GRUSHA *dashes at him to pull him away. He throws her off and again bends over the crib. Again looking round in despair, she sees a log of wood, seizes it, and hits the* CORPORAL *over the head from behind. The* CORPORAL *collapses. She quickly picks up the* CHILD *and rushes off.*]

THE SINGER:
And in her flight from the Ironshirts
After twenty-two days of journeying
At the foot of the Janga Tau Glacier
Grusha Vashnadze decided to adopt the child.

THE CHORUS:
The helpless girl adopted the helpless child.
[GRUSHA *squats over a half-frozen stream to get the* CHILD *water in the hollow of her hand.*]

GRUSHA:
Since no one else will take you, son,
I must take you.
Since no one else will take you, son,

You must take me.
O black day in a lean, lean year,
The trip was long, the milk was dear,
My legs are tired, my feet are sore:
But I wouldn't be without you any more.
I'll throw your silken shirt away
And dress you in rags and tatters.
I'll wash you, son, and christen you in glacier water.
We'll see it through together.

[*She has taken off the child's fine linen and wrapped it in a rag.*]

THE SINGER:
When Grusha Vashnadze
Pursued by the Ironshirts
Came to the bridge on the glacier
Leading to the villages of the Eastern Slope
She sang the Song of the Rotten Bridge
And risked two lives.

[*A wind has risen. The bridge on the glacier is visible in the dark. One rope is broken and half the bridge is hanging down the abyss.* MERCHANTS, *two men and a woman, stand undecided before the bridge as* GRUSHA *and the* CHILD *arrive.* ONE MAN *is trying to catch the hanging rope with a stick.*]

THE FIRST MAN: Take your time, young woman. You won't get across here anyway.

GRUSHA: But I *have* to get the baby to the east side. To my brother's place.

THE MERCHANT WOMAN: Have to? How d'you mean, 'have to'? I have to get there, too – because I have to buy carpets in Atum – carpets a woman had to sell because her husband had to die. But can *I* do what I have to? Can she? Andrei's been fishing for that rope for hours. And I ask you, how are we going to fasten it, even if he gets it up?

THE FIRST MAN [*listening*]: Hush, I think I hear something.

GRUSHA: The bridge isn't quite rotted through. I think I'll try it.

THE MERCHANT WOMAN: *I* wouldn't – if the devil himself were after me. It's suicide.

THE FIRST MAN [*shouting*]: Hi!

GRUSHA: Don't shout! [*To the* MERCHANT WOMAN] Tell him not to shout.

THE FIRST MAN: But there's someone down there calling. Maybe they've lost their way.

THE MERCHANT WOMAN: Why shouldn't he shout? Is there something funny about you? Are they after you?

GRUSHA: All right, I'll tell. The Ironshirts are after me. I knocked one down.

THE SECOND MAN: Hide our merchandise! [*The* WOMAN *hides a sack behind a rock.*]

THE FIRST MAN: Why didn't you say so right away? [*To the others*] If they catch her they'll make mincemeat out of her!

GRUSHA: Get out of my way. I've got to cross that bridge.

THE SECOND MAN: You can't. The precipice is two thousand feet deep.

THE FIRST MAN: Even with the rope it'd be no use. We could hold it up with our hands. But then we'd have to do the same for the Ironshirts.

GRUSHA: Go away.

[*There are calls from the distance:* 'Hi, up there!']

THE MERCHANT WOMAN: They're getting near. But you can't take the child on that bridge. It's sure to break. And look!

[GRUSHA *looks down into the abyss. The* IRONSHIRTS *are heard calling again from below.*]

THE SECOND MAN: Two thousand feet!

GRUSHA: But those men are worse.

THE FIRST MAN: You can't do it. Think of the baby. Risk your life but not a child's.

THE SECOND MAN: With the child she's that much heavier!

THE MERCHANT WOMAN: Maybe she's *really* got to get across. Give *me* the baby. I'll hide it. Cross the bridge alone!

GRUSHA: I won't. We belong together. [*To the* CHILD] 'Live together, die together.' [*She sings.*]

THE SONG OF THE ROTTEN BRIDGE

Deep is the abyss, son,
I see the weak bridge sway
But it's not for us, son,
To choose the way.

The way I know
Is the one you must tread,
And all you will eat
Is my bit of bread.

Of every four pieces
You shall have three.
Would that I knew
How big they will be!

Get out of my way, I'll try it without the rope.

THE MERCHANT WOMAN: You are tempting God!

[*There are shouts from below.*]

GRUSHA: Please, throw that stick away, or they'll get the rope and follow me. [*Pressing the* CHILD *to her, she steps onto the swaying bridge. The* MERCHANT WOMAN *screams when it looks as though the bridge is about to collapse. But* GRUSHA *walks on and reaches the far side.*]

THE FIRST MAN: She made it!

THE MERCHANT WOMAN [*who has fallen on her knees and begun to pray, angrily*]: I still think it was a sin.

[*The* IRONSHIRTS *appear; the* CORPORAL'S *head is bandaged.*]

THE CORPORAL: Seen a woman with a child?

THE FIRST MAN [*while the* SECOND MAN *throws the stick into the abyss*]: Yes, there! But the bridge won't carry you!

THE CORPORAL: You'll pay for this, blockhead!

    [GRUSHA, *from the far bank, laughs and shows the* CHILD *to the* IRONSHIRTS. *She walks on. The wind blows.*]

GRUSHA [*turning to the* CHILD]: You mustn't be afraid of the wind. He's a poor thing too. He has to push the clouds along and he gets quite cold doing it. [*Snow starts falling.*] And the snow isn't so bad, either, Michael. It covers the little fir trees so they won't die in winter. Let me sing you a little song. [*She sings.*]

THE SONG OF THE CHILD

Your father is a bandit.
A harlot the mother who bore you.
Yet honourable men
Shall kneel down before you.

Food to the baby horses
The tiger's son will take.
The mothers will get milk
From the son of the snake.

3. In the Northern Mountains

THE SINGER:

Seven days the sister, Grusha Vashnadze,
Journeyed across the glacier
And down the slopes she journeyed.
'When I enter my brother's house,' she thought,
'He will rise and embrace me.'
'Is that you, sister?' he will say,
'I have long expected you.
This is my dear wife,
And this is my farm, come to me by marriage,
With eleven horses and thirty-one cows. Sit down.
Sit down with your child at our table and eat.'

The brother's house was in a lovely valley.
When the sister came to the brother,
She was ill from walking.
The brother rose from the table.

[*A* FAT PEASANT COUPLE *rise from the table.* LAVRENTI
VASHNADZE *still has a napkin round his neck, as* GRUSHA,
pale and supported by a SERVANT, *enters with the* CHILD.]

LAVRENTI: Where've *you* come from, Grusha?

GRUSHA [*feebly*]: Across the Janga Tau Pass, Lavrenti.

THE SERVANT: I found her in front of the hay barn. She has a
baby with her.

THE SISTER-IN-LAW: Go and groom the mare. [*Exit the*
SERVANT.]

LAVRENTI: This is my wife Aniko.

THE SISTER-IN-LAW: I thought you were in service in Nuka.

GRUSHA [*barely able to stand*]: Yes, I was.

THE SISTER-IN-LAW: Wasn't it a good job? We were told it
was.

GRUSHA: The Governor got killed.

LAVRENTI: Yes, we heard there were riots. Your aunt told
us. Remember, Aniko?

THE SISTER-IN-LAW: Here with us, it's very quiet. City
people always want something going on. [*She walks toward
the door, calling.*] Sosso, Sosso, don't take the cake out of the
oven yet, d'you hear? Where on earth are you? [*Exit,
calling.*]

LAVRENTI [*quietly, quickly*]: Is there a father? [*As she shakes her
head*] I thought not. We must think up something. She's
religious.

THE SISTER-IN-LAW [*returning*]: Those servants! [*To
GRUSHA*] You have a child.

GRUSHA: It's mine. [*She collapses.* LAVRENTI *rushes to her
assistance.*]

THE SISTER-IN-LAW: Heavens, she's ill – what are we going
to do?

LAVRENTI [*escorting her to a bench near the stove*]: Sit down, sit. I think it's just weakness, Aniko.

THE SISTER-IN-LAW: As long as it's not scarlet fever!

LAVRENTI: She'd have spots if it was. It's only weakness. Don't worry, Aniko. [*To* GRUSHA] Better, sitting down?

THE SISTER-IN-LAW: Is the child hers?

GRUSHA: Yes, mine.

LAVRENTI: She's on her way to her husband.

THE SISTER-IN-LAW: I see. Your meat's getting cold. [LAVRENTI *sits down and begins to eat.*] Cold food's not good for you, the fat mustn't get cold, you know your stomach's your weak spot. [*To* GRUSHA] If your husband's not in the city, where is he?

LAVRENTI: She got married on the other side of the mountain, she says.

THE SISTER-IN-LAW: On the other side of the mountain. I see. [*She also sits down to eat.*]

GRUSHA: I think I should lie down somewhere, Lavrenti.

THE SISTER-IN-LAW: If it's consumption we'll all get it. [*She goes on cross-examining her.*] Has your husband got a farm?

GRUSHA: He's a soldier.

LAVRENTI: But he's coming into a farm – a small one – from his father.

THE SISTER-IN-LAW: Isn't he in the war? Why not?

GRUSHA [*with effort*]: Yes, he's in the war.

THE SISTER-IN-LAW: Then why d'you want to go to the farm?

LAVRENTI: When he comes back from the war, he'll return to his farm.

THE SISTER-IN-LAW: But you're going there now?

LAVRENTI: Yes, to wait for him.

THE SISTER-IN-LAW [*calling shrilly*]: Sosso, the cake!

GRUSHA [*murmuring feverishly*]: A farm – a soldier – waiting – sit down, eat.

THE SISTER-IN-LAW: It's scarlet fever.

GRUSHA [*starting up*]: Yes, he's got a farm!

LAVRENTI: I think it's just weakness, Aniko. Would you look after the cake yourself, dear?

THE SISTER-IN-LAW: But when will he come back if war's broken out again as people say? [*She waddles off, shouting*] Sosso! Where on earth are you? Sosso!

LAVRENTI [*getting up quickly and going to* GRUSHA]: You'll get a bed in a minute. She has a good heart. But wait till after supper.

GRUSHA [*holding out the* CHILD *to him*]: Take him.

LAVRENTI [*taking it and looking around*]: But you can't stay here long with the child. She's religious, you see. [GRUSHA *collapses.* LAVRENTI *catches her.*]

THE SINGER:

The sister was so ill,
The cowardly brother had to give her shelter.
Summer departed, winter came.
The winter was long, the winter was short
People mustn't know anything,
Rats mustn't bite,
Spring mustn't come.

[GRUSHA *sits over the weaving loom in a workroom. She and the* CHILD, *who is squatting on the floor, are wrapped in blankets. She sings.*]

THE SONG OF THE CENTRE

And the lover started to leave
And his betrothed ran pleading after him
Pleading and weeping, weeping and teaching:
'Dearest mine, dearest mine
When you go to war as now you do
When you fight the foe as soon you will
Don't lead with the front line
And don't push with the rear line
At the front is red fire

In the rear is red smoke
Stay in the war's centre
Stay near the standard bearer
The first always die
The last are also hit
Those in the centre come home.'

Michael, we must be clever. If we make ourselves as small as cockroaches, the sister-in-law will forget we're in the house, and then we can stay till the snow melts.

[*Enter* LAVRENTI. *He sits down beside his* SISTER.]

LAVRENTI: Why are you sitting there muffled up like coachmen, you two? Is it too cold in the room?

GRUSHA [*hastily removing one shawl*]: It's not too cold, Lavrenti.

LAVRENTI: If it's too cold, you shouldn't be sitting here with the child. Aniko would never forgive herself! [*Pause.*] I hope our priest didn't question you about the child?

GRUSHA: He did, but I didn't tell him anything.

LAVRENTI: That's good. I wanted to speak to you about Aniko. She has a good heart but she's very, very sensitive. People need only mention our farm and she's worried. She takes everything hard, you see. One time our milkmaid went to church with a hole in her stocking. Ever since, Aniko has worn two pairs of stockings in church. It's the old family in her. [*He listens.*] Are you sure there are no rats around? If there are rats, you couldn't live here. [*There are sounds as of dripping from the roof.*] What's that, dripping?

GRUSHA: It must be a barrel leaking.

LAVRENTI: Yes, it must be a barrel. You've been here six months, haven't you? Was I talking about Aniko? [*They listen again to the snow melting.*] You can't imagine how worried she gets about your soldier-husband. 'Suppose he comes back and can't find her!' she says and lies awake. 'He can't come before the spring,' I tell her. The dear woman! [*The drops begin to fall faster.*] When d'you think he'll come? What do *you* think? [GRUSHA *is silent.*] Not before the spring, you agree? [GRUSHA *is silent.*] You don't believe he'll come at all? [GRUSHA *is silent.*] But when the spring comes and the snow melts here and on the passes, you can't stay on. They may come and look for you. There's already talk of an illegitimate child. [*The 'glockenspiel' of the falling drops has grown faster and steadier.*] Grusha, the snow is melting on the roof. Spring is here.

GRUSHA: Yes.

LAVRENTI [*eagerly*]: I'll tell you what we'll do. You need a place to go, and, because of the child [*he sighs*], you have to have a husband, so people won't talk. Now I've made cautious inquiries to see if we can find you a husband. Grusha, I *have* one. I talked to a peasant woman who has a son. Just the other side of the mountain. A small farm. And she's willing.

GRUSHA: But I *can't* marry! I must wait for Simon Shashava.

LAVRENTI: Of course. That's all been taken care of. You don't need a man in bed – you need a man on paper. And I've found you one. The son of this peasant woman is going to die. Isn't that wonderful? He's at his last gasp. And all in line with our story – a husband from the other side of the mountain! And when you met him he was at the last gasp. So you're a widow. What do you say?

GRUSHA: It's true I could use a document with stamps on it for Michael.

LAVRENTI: Stamps make all the difference. Without something in writing the Shah couldn't prove he's a Shah. And you'll have a place to live.

GRUSHA: How much does the peasant woman want?

LAVRENTI: Four hundred piastres.

GRUSHA: Where will you find it?

LAVRENTI [*guiltily*]: Aniko's milk money.

GRUSHA: No one would know us there. I'll do it.

LAVRENTI [*getting up*]: I'll let the peasant woman know. [*Quick exit.*]

GRUSHA: Michael, you cause a lot of fuss. I came to you as the pear tree comes to the sparrows. And because a Christian bends down and picks up a crust of bread so nothing will go to waste. Michael, it would have been better had I walked quickly away on that Easter Sunday in Nuka in the second courtyard. Now I *am* a fool.

THE SINGER:

The bridegroom was on his deathbed when the bride arrived.

The bridegroom's mother was waiting at the door, telling her to hurry.

The bride brought a child along.

The witness hid it during the wedding.

[*On one side the bed. Under the mosquito net lies a very sick* MAN. GRUSHA *is pulled in at a run by her future* MOTHER-IN-LAW. *They are followed by* LAVRENTI *and the* CHILD.]

THE MOTHER-IN-LAW: Quick! Quick! Or he'll die on us before the wedding. [*To* LAVRENTI] I was never told she had a child already.

LAVRENTI: What difference does it make? [*Pointing toward the* DYING MAN] It can't matter to him – in his condition.

THE MOTHER-IN-LAW: To him? But I'll never survive the shame! We are honest people. [*She begins to weep.*] My Jussup doesn't have to marry a girl with a child!

LAVRENTI: All right, make it another two hundred piastres. You'll have it in writing that the farm will go to you: but she'll have the right to live here for two years.

THE MOTHER-IN-LAW [*drying her tears*]: It'll hardly cover the funeral expenses. I hope she'll really lend a hand with the work. And what's happened to the monk? He must have slipped out through the kitchen window. We'll have the whole village on our necks when they hear Jussup's end is come! Oh dear! I'll go get the monk. But he mustn't see the child!

LAVRENTI: I'll take care he doesn't. But why only a monk? Why not a priest?

THE MOTHER-IN-LAW: Oh, he's just as good. I only made one mistake: I paid half his fee in advance. Enough to send him to the tavern. I only hope . . . [*She runs off.*]

LAVRENTI: She saved on the priest, the wretch! Hired a cheap monk.

GRUSHA: You *will* send Simon Shashava to see me if he turns up after all?

LAVRENTI: Yes. [*Pointing at the* SICK MAN] Won't you take a look at him? [GRUSHA, *taking* MICHAEL *to her, shakes her head.*] He's not moving an eyelid. I hope we aren't too late.

[*They listen. On the opposite side enter* NEIGHBOURS *who look around and take up positions against the walls, thus forming another wall near the bed, yet leaving an opening so that the bed can be seen. They start murmuring prayers. Enter the* MOTHER-IN-LAW *with a* MONK. *Showing some annoyance and surprise she bows to the* GUESTS.]

THE MOTHER-IN-LAW: I hope you won't mind waiting a few moments? My son's bride has just arrived from the city. An emergency wedding is about to be celebrated. [*To the* MONK *in the bedroom*] I might have known you couldn't keep your trap shut. [*To* GRUSHA] The wedding can take place at once. Here's the licence. Me and the bride's brother [LAVRENTI *tries to hide in the background, after having quietly taken* MICHAEL *back from* GRUSHA. *The* MOTHER-IN-LAW *waves him away*] are the witnesses.

[GRUSHA *has bowed to the* MONK. *They go to the bed. The* MOTHER-IN-LAW *lifts the mosquito net. The* MONK *starts reeling off the marriage ceremony in Latin. Meanwhile, the* MOTHER-IN-LAW *beckons to* LAVRENTI *to get rid of the* CHILD, *but fearing that it will cry he draws its attention to the*

ceremony. GRUSHA *glances once at the* CHILD, *and* LAV-
RENTI *waves the* CHILD'S *hand in a greeting.*]

THE MONK: Are you prepared to be a faithful, obedient, and
good wife to this man, and to cleave to him until death you
do part?

GRUSHA [*looking at the* CHILD]: I am.

THE MONK [*to the* SICK PEASANT]: Are you prepared to be a
good and loving husband to your wife until death you do
part? [*As the* SICK PEASANT *does not answer, the* MONK *looks
inquiringly around.*]

THE MOTHER-IN-LAW: Of course he is! Didn't you hear him
say yes?

THE MONK: All right. We declare the marriage contracted!
How about extreme unction?

THE MOTHER-IN-LAW: Nothing doing! The wedding cost
quite enough. Now I must take care of the mourners. [*To*
LAVRENTI] Did we say seven hundred?

LAVRENTI: Six hundred. [*He pays.*] Now I don't want to sit
with the guests and get to know people. So farewell, Grusha,
and if my widowed sister comes to visit me, she'll get a
welcome from my wife, or I'll show my teeth. [*Nods, gives
the* CHILD *to* GRUSHA, *and leaves. The* MOURNERS *glance
after him without interest.*]

THE MONK: May one ask where this child comes from?

THE MOTHER-IN-LAW: Is there a child? I don't see a child.
And you don't see a child either – you understand? Or it
may turn out I saw all sorts of things in the tavern! Now
come on. [*After* GRUSHA *has put the* CHILD *down and told him
to be quiet, they move over left.* GRUSHA *is introduced to the*
NEIGHBOURS.] This is my daughter-in-law. She arrived
just in time to find dear Jussup still alive.

ONE WOMAN: He's been ill now a whole year, hasn't he?
When our Vassili was drafted he was there to say good-
bye.

ANOTHER WOMAN: Such things are terrible for a farm. The

corn all ripe and the farmer in bed! It'll really be a blessing if he doesn't suffer too long, I say.

THE FIRST WOMAN [*confidentially*]: You know why we thought he'd taken to his bed? Because of the draft! And now his end is come!

THE MOTHER-IN-LAW: Sit yourselves down, please! And have some cakes! [*She beckons to* GRUSHA *and* BOTH WOMEN *go into the bedroom, where they pick up the cake pans off the floor.*]
[*The* GUESTS, *among them the* MONK, *sit on the floor and begin conversing in subdued voices.*]

ONE PEASANT [*to whom the* MONK *has handed the bottle which he has taken from his soutane*]: There's a child, you say! How can that have happened to Jussup?

A WOMAN: She was certainly lucky to get herself hitched, with him so sick!

THE MOTHER-IN-LAW: They're gossiping already. And wolfing down the funeral cakes at the same time! If he doesn't die today, I'll have to bake some more tomorrow!

GRUSHA: I'll bake them for you.

THE MOTHER-IN-LAW: Yesterday some horsemen rode by, and I went out to see who it was. When I came in again he was lying there like a corpse! So I sent for you. It can't take much longer. [*She listens.*]

THE MONK: Dear wedding and funeral guests! Deeply touched, we stand before a bed of death and marriage. The bride gets a veil; the groom, a shroud: how varied, my children, are the fates of men! Alas! One man dies and has a roof over his head and the other is married and the flesh turns to dust from which it was made. Amen.

THE MOTHER-IN-LAW: He's getting his own back. I shouldn't have hired such a cheap one. It's what you'd expect. A more expensive monk would behave himself. In Sura there's one with a real air of sanctity about him, but of course he charges a fortune. A fifty-piastre monk like that has no dignity, and as for piety, just fifty piastres' worth and no more! When I

came to get him in the tavern he'd just made a speech, and
he was shouting: 'The war is over, beware of the peace!'
We must go in.

GRUSHA [*giving* MICHAEL *a cake*]: Eat this cake, and keep nice
and still, Michael.

[*The* TWO WOMEN *offer cakes to the* GUESTS. *The* DYING
MAN *sits up in bed. He puts his head out from under the mosquito net, stares at the* TWO WOMEN, *then sinks back again.
The* MONK *takes two bottles from his soutane and offers them
to the* PEASANT *beside him. Enter* THREE MUSICIANS *who
are greeted with a sly wink by the* MONK.]

THE MOTHER-IN-LAW [*to the* MUSICIANS]: What are you
doing here? With instruments?

ONE MUSICIAN: Brother Anastasius here [*pointing at the*
MONK] told us there was a wedding on.

THE MOTHER-IN-LAW: What? You brought them? Three
more on my neck! Don't you know there's a dying man in
the next room?

THE MONK: A very tempting assignment for a musician:
something that could be either a subdued Wedding March
or a spirited Funeral Dance.

THE MOTHER-IN-LAW: Well, you might as well play. Nobody can stop you eating in any case.

[*The* MUSICIANS *play a potpourri. The* WOMEN *serve
cakes.*]

THE MONK: The trumpet sounds like a whining baby. And
you, little drum, what have you got to tell the world?

THE DRUNKEN PEASANT [*beside the* MONK, *sings*]:
　　　Miss Roundass took the old old man
　　　And said that marriage was the thing
　　　To everyone who met 'er.
　　　She later withdrew from the contract because
　　　Candles are better.

[*The* MOTHER-IN-LAW *throws the* DRUNKEN PEASANT
out. The music stops. The GUESTS *are embarrassed.*]

THE GUESTS [*loudly*]: Have you heard? The Grand Duke is back! But the Princes are against him.

– They say the Shah of Persia has lent him a great army to restore order in Grusinia.

– But how is that possible? The Shah of Persia is the enemy ...

– The enemy of Grusinia, you donkey, not the enemy of the Grand Duke!

– In any case, the war's over, so our soldiers are coming back. [GRUSHA *drops a cake pan.* GUESTS *help her pick up the cake.*]

AN OLD WOMAN [*to* GRUSHA]: Are you feeling bad? It's just excitement about dear Jussup. Sit down and rest a while, my dear. [GRUSHA *staggers.*]

THE GUESTS: Now everything'll be the way it was. Only the taxes'll go up because now we'll have to pay for the war.

GRUSHA [*weakly*]: Did someone say the soldiers are back?

A MAN: I did.

GRUSHA: It can't be true.

THE FIRST MAN [*to a* WOMAN]: Show her the shawl. We bought it from a soldier. It's from Persia.

GRUSHA [*looking at the shawl*]: They are here. [*She gets up, takes a step, kneels down in prayer, takes the silver cross and chain out of her blouse, and kisses it.*]

THE MOTHER-IN-LAW [*while the* GUESTS *silently watch* GRUSHA]: What's the matter with you? Aren't you going to look after our guests? What's all this city nonsense got to do with us?

THE GUESTS [*resuming conversation while* GRUSHA *remains in prayer*]: You can buy Persian saddles from the soldiers too. Though many want crutches in exchange for them.

– The big shots on one side can win a war, the soldiers on both sides lose it.

– Anyway, the war's over. It's something they can't draft you any more.

[*The* DYING MAN *sits bolt upright in bed. He listens.*]

– What we need is two weeks of good weather.

– Our pear trees are hardly bearing a thing this year.

THE MOTHER-IN-LAW [*offering cakes*]: Have some more cakes and welcome! There are more! [*Goes to the bedroom with the empty cake pans. Unaware of the* DYING MAN, *she is bending down to pick up another tray when he begins to talk in a hoarse voice.*]

THE PEASANT: How many more cakes are you going to stuff down their throats? D'you think I can shit money?

[*The* MOTHER-IN-LAW *starts, stares at him aghast, while he climbs out from behind the mosquito net.*]

THE FIRST WOMAN [*talking kindly to* GRUSHA *in the next room*]: Has the young wife got someone at the front?

A MAN: It's good news that they're on their way home, huh?

THE PEASANT: Don't stare at me like that! Where's this wife you've saddled me with? [*Receiving no answer, he climbs out of bed and in his nightshirt staggers into the other room. Trembling, she follows him with the cake pan.*]

THE GUESTS [*seeing him and shrieking*]: Good God! Jussup!

[*Everyone leaps up in alarm. The* WOMEN *rush to the door.* GRUSHA, *still on her knees, turns round and stares at the* MAN.]

THE PEASANT: A funeral supper! You'd enjoy that, wouldn't you? Get out before I throw you out! [*As the* GUESTS *stampede from the house, gloomily to* GRUSHA] I've upset the apple cart, huh? [*Receiving no answer, he turns round and takes a cake from the pan which his mother is holding.*]

THE SINGER:

O confusion! The wife discovers she has a husband.

By day there's the child, by night there's the husband.

The lover is on his way both day and night.

Husband and wife look at each other.

The bedroom is small.

[*Near the bed the* PEASANT *is sitting in a high wooden bathtub, naked, the* MOTHER-IN-LAW *is pouring water from a pitcher. Opposite* GRUSHA *cowers with* MICHAEL, *who is playing at mending straw mats.*]

THE PEASANT [*to his* MOTHER]: That's her work, not yours.
Where's she hiding out now?

THE MOTHER-IN-LAW [*calling*]: Grusha! The peasant wants
you!

GRUSHA [*to* MICHAEL]: There are still two holes to mend.

THE PEASANT [*when* GRUSHA *approaches*]: Scrub my back!

GRUSHA: Can't the peasant do it himself?

THE PEASANT: 'Can't the peasant do it himself?' Get the brush!
To hell with you! Are you the wife here? Or are you a visitor? [*To the* MOTHER-IN-LAW] It's too cold!

THE MOTHER-IN-LAW: I'll run for hot water.

GRUSHA: Let me go.

THE PEASANT: You stay here. [*The* MOTHER-IN-LAW *exits.*]
Rub harder. And no shirking. You've seen a naked fellow
before. That child didn't come out of thin air.

GRUSHA: The child was not conceived in joy, if that's what the
peasant means.

THE PEASANT [*turning and grinning*]: You don't look the type.
[GRUSHA *stops scrubbing him, starts back. Enter the* MOTHER-
IN-LAW.]

THE PEASANT: A nice thing you've saddled me with! A simpleton for a wife!

THE MOTHER-IN-LAW: She just isn't cooperative.

THE PEASANT: Pour – but go easy! Ow! Go easy, I said. [*To*
GRUSHA] Maybe you did something wrong in the city . . .
I wouldn't be surprised. Why else should you be here? But
I won't talk about that. I've not said a word about the ille-
gitimate object you brought into my house either. But my
patience has limits! It's against nature. [*To the* MOTHER-IN-
LAW] More! [*To* GRUSHA] And even if your soldier does
come back, you're married.

GRUSHA: Yes.

THE PEASANT: But your soldier won't come back. Don't you
believe it.

GRUSHA: No.

THE PEASANT: You're cheating me. You're my wife and you're not my wife. Where you lie, nothing lies, and yet no other woman can lie there. When I go to work in the morning I'm tired – when I lie down at night I'm awake as the devil. God has given you sex – and what d'you do? I don't have ten piastres to buy myself a woman in the city. Besides, it's a long way. Woman weeds the fields and opens up her legs, that's what our calendar says. D'you hear?

GRUSHA [*quietly*]: Yes. I didn't mean to cheat you out of it.

THE PEASANT: She didn't mean to cheat me out of it! Pour some more water! [*The* MOTHER-IN-LAW *pours.*] Ow!

THE SINGER:
As she sat by the stream to wash the linen
She saw his image in the water
And his face grew dimmer with the passing moons.
As she raised herself to wring the linen
She heard his voice from the murmuring maple
And his voice grew fainter with the passing moons.
Evasions and sighs grew more numerous,
Tears and sweat flowed.
With the passing moons the child grew up.

[GRUSHA *sits by a stream, dipping linen into the water. In the rear, a few* CHILDREN *are standing.*]

GRUSHA [*to* MICHAEL]: You can play with them, Michael, but don't let them boss you around just because you're the littlest.

[MICHAEL *nods and joins the* CHILDREN. *They start playing.*]

THE BIGGEST BOY: Today it's the Heads-Off Game. [*To a* FAT BOY] You're the Prince and you laugh. [*To* MICHAEL] You're the Governor. [*To a* GIRL] You're the Governor's wife and you cry when his head's cut off. And I do the cutting. [*He shows his wooden sword*] With this. First, they lead the Governor into the yard. The Prince walks in front. The Governor's wife comes last.

[*They form a procession. The* FAT BOY *is first and laughs. Then comes* MICHAEL, *then the* BIGGEST BOY, *and then the* GIRL, *who weeps.*]

MICHAEL [*standing still*]: Me cut off head!

THE BIGGEST BOY: That's my job. You're the littlest. The Governor's the easy part. All you do is kneel down and get your head cut off – simple.

MICHAEL: Me want sword!

THE BIGGEST BOY: It's mine! [*He gives him a kick.*]

THE GIRL [*shouting to* GRUSHA]: He won't play his part!

GRUSHA [*laughing*]: Even the little duck is a swimmer, they say.

THE BIGGEST BOY: You can be the Prince if you can laugh. [MICHAEL *shakes his head.*]

THE FAT BOY: I laugh best. Let him cut off the head just once. Then you do it, then me.

[*Reluctantly, the* BIGGEST BOY *hands* MICHAEL *the wooden sword and kneels down. The* FAT BOY *sits down, slaps his thigh, and laughs with all his might. The* GIRL *weeps loudly.* MICHAEL *swings the big sword and 'cuts off' the head. In doing so, he topples over.*]

THE BIGGEST BOY: Hey! I'll show you how to cut heads off! [MICHAEL *runs away. The* CHILDREN *run after him.* GRUSHA *laughs, following them with her eyes. On looking back, she sees* SIMON SHASHAVA *standing on the opposite bank. He wears a shabby uniform.*]

GRUSHA: Simon!

SIMON: Is that Grusha Vashnadze?

GRUSHA. Simon.

SIMON [*formally*]: A good morning to the young lady. I hope she is well.

GRUSHA [*getting up gaily and bowing low*]: A good morning to the soldier. God be thanked he has returned in good health.

SIMON: They found better fish, so they didn't eat me, said the haddock.

GRUSHA: Courage, said the kitchen boy. Good luck, said the hero.

SIMON: How are things here? Was the winter bearable? The neighbour considerate?

GRUSHA: The winter was a trifle rough, the neighbour as usual, Simon.

SIMON: May one ask if a certain person still dips her toes in the water when rinsing the linen?

GRUSHA: The answer is no. Because of the eyes in the bushes.

SIMON: The young lady is speaking of soldiers. Here stands a paymaster.

GRUSHA: A job worth twenty piastres?

SIMON: And lodgings.

GRUSHA [with tears in her eyes]: Behind the barracks under the date trees.

SIMON: Yes, there. A certain person has kept her eyes open.

GRUSHA: She has, Simon.

SIMON: And has not forgotten? [GRUSHA shakes her head.] So the door is still on its hinges as they say? [GRUSHA looks at him in silence and shakes her head again.] What's this? Is anything not as it should be?

GRUSHA: Simon Shashava, I can never return to Nuka. Something has happened.

SIMON: What can have happened?

GRUSHA: For one thing, I knocked an Ironshirt down.

SIMON: Grusha Vashnadze must have had her reasons for that.

GRUSHA: Simon Shashava, I am no longer called what I used to be called.

SIMON [after a pause]: I do not understand.

GRUSHA: When do women change their names, Simon? Let me explain. Nothing stands between us. Everything is just as it was. You must believe that.

SIMON: Nothing stands between us and yet there's something?

GRUSHA: How can I explain it so fast and with the stream between us? Couldn't you cross the bridge there?

SIMON: Maybe it's no longer necessary.

GRUSHA: It is very necessary. Come over on this side, Simon. Quick!

SIMON: Does the young lady wish to say someone has come too late?

> [GRUSHA *looks up at him in despair, her face streaming with tears.* SIMON *stares before him. He picks up a piece of wood and starts cutting it.*]

THE SINGER:

> So many words are said, so many left unsaid.
>
> The soldier has come.
>
> Where he comes from, he does not say.
>
> Hear what he thought and did not say:
>
> 'The battle began, grey at dawn, grew bloody at noon.
>
> The first man fell in front of me, the second behind me, the third at my side.
>
> I trod on the first, left the second behind, the third was run through by the captain.
>
> One of my brothers died by steel, the other by smoke.
>
> My neck caught fire, my hands froze in my gloves, my toes in my socks.
>
> I fed on aspen buds, I drank maple juice, I slept on stone, in water.'

SIMON: I see a cap in the grass. Is there a little one already?

GRUSHA: There is, Simon. There's no keeping *that* from you. But please don't worry, it is not mine.

SIMON: When the wind once starts to blow, they say, it blows through every cranny. The wife need say no more. [GRUSHA *looks into her lap and is silent.*]

THE SINGER:

> There was yearning but there was no waiting.
>
> The oath is broken. Neither could say why.
>
> Hear what she thought but did not say:
>
> 'While you fought in the battle, soldier,
>
> The bloody battle, the bitter battle

I found a helpless infant
I had not the heart to destroy him
I had to care for a creature that was lost
I had to stoop for breadcrumbs on the floor
I had to break myself for that which was not mine
That which was other people's.
Someone must help!
For the little tree needs water
The lamb loses its way when the shepherd is asleep
And its cry is unheard!'

SIMON: Give me back the cross I gave you. Better still, throw it in the stream. [*He turns to go.*]

GRUSHA [*getting up*]: Simon Shashava, don't go away! He isn't mine! He isn't mine! [*She hears the* CHILDREN *calling.*] What's the matter, children?

VOICES: Soldiers! And they're taking Michael away!

[GRUSHA *stands aghast as* TWO IRONSHIRTS, *with* MICHAEL *between them, come toward her.*]

ONE OF THE IRONSHIRTS: Are you Grusha? [*She nods.*] Is this your child?

GRUSHA: Yes. [SIMON *goes.*] Simon!

THE IRONSHIRT: We have orders, in the name of the law, to take this child, found in your custody, back to the city. It is suspected that the child is Michael Abashwili, son and heir of the late Governor Georgi Abashwili, and his wife, Natella Abashwili. Here is the document and the seal. [*They lead the* CHILD *away.*]

GRUSHA [*running after them, shouting*]: Leave him here. Please! He's mine!

THE SINGER:
The Ironshirts took the child, the beloved child.
The unhappy girl followed them to the city, the dreaded city.
She who had borne him demanded the child.
She who had raised him faced trial.

Who will decide the case?
To whom will the child be assigned?
Who will the judge be? A good judge? A bad?
The city was in flames.
In the judge's seat sat Azdak.*

4. The Story of the Judge

THE SINGER:
Hear the story of the judge
How he turned judge, how he passed judgment, what kind
of judge he was.
On that Easter Sunday of the great revolt, when the Grand
Duke was overthrown
And his Governor Abashwili, father of our child, lost his
head
The Village Scrivener Azdak found a fugitive in the woods
and hid him in his hut.

[AZDAK, *in rags and slightly drunk, is helping an* OLD BEG-
GAR *into his cottage.*]

AZDAK: Stop snorting, you're not a horse. And it won't do
you any good with the police to run like a snotty nose in
April. Stand still, I say. [*He catches the* OLD MAN, *who has
marched into the cottage as if he'd like to go through the walls.*]
Sit down. Feed. Here's a hunk of cheese. [*From under some
rags, in a chest, he fishes out some cheese, and the* OLD MAN
greedily begins to eat.] Haven't eaten in a long time, huh? [*The*
OLD MAN *growls.*] Why were you running like that, asshole?
The cop wouldn't even have seen you.

THE OLD MAN: Had to! Had to!

AZDAK: Blue funk? [*The* OLD MAN *stares, uncomprehending.*]
Cold feet? Panic? Don't lick your chops like a Grand Duke.

* The name Azdak should be accented on the second syllable. E.B.

Or an old sow. I can't stand it. We have to accept respectable stinkers as God made them, but not you! I once heard of a senior judge who farted at a public dinner to show an independent spirit! Watching you eat like that gives me the most awful ideas. Why don't you say something? [*Sharply.*] Show me your hand. Can't you hear? [*The* OLD MAN *slowly puts out his hand.*] White! So you're not a beggar at all! A fraud, a walking swindle! And I'm hiding you from the cops like you were an honest man! Why were you running like that if you're a landowner? For that's what you are. Don't deny it! I see it in your guilty face! [*He gets up.*] Get out! [*The* OLD MAN *looks at him uncertainly.*] What are you waiting for, peasant-flogger?

THE OLD MAN: Pursued. Need undivided attention. Make proposition . . .

AZDAK: Make what? A proposition? Well, if that isn't the height of insolence. He's making me a proposition! The bitten man scratches his fingers bloody, and the leech that's biting him makes him a proposition! Get out, I tell you!

THE OLD MAN: Understand point of view! Persuasion! Pay hundred thousand piastres one night! Yes?

AZDAK: What, you think you can buy me? For a hundred thousand piastres? Let's say a hundred and fifty thousand. Where are they?

THE OLD MAN: Have not them here. Of course. Will be sent. Hope do not doubt.

AZDAK: Doubt very much. Get out!

[*The* OLD MAN *gets up, waddles to the door. A* VOICE *is heard off-stage.*]

A VOICE: Azdak!

[*The* OLD MAN *turns, waddles to the opposite corner, stands still.*]

AZDAK [*calling out*]: I'm not in! [*He walks to door.*] So you're sniffing around here again, Shauwa?

POLICEMAN SHAUWA [*reproachfully*]: You caught another

rabbit, Azdak. And you'd promised me it wouldn't happen again!

AZDAK [*severely*]: Shauwa, don't talk about things you don't understand. The rabbit is a dangerous and destructive beast. It feeds on plants, especially on the species of plants known as weeds. It must therefore be exterminated.

SHAUWA: Azdak, don't be so hard on me. I'll lose my job if I don't arrest you. I know you have a good heart.

AZDAK: I do not have a good heart! How often must I tell you I'm a man of intellect?

SHAUWA [*slyly*]: I know, Azdak. You're a superior person. You say so yourself. I'm just a Christian and an ignoramus. So I ask you: When one of the Prince's rabbits is stolen, and I'm a policeman, what should I do with the offending party?

AZDAK: Shauwa, Shauwa, shame on you. You stand and ask me a question, than which nothing could be more seductive. It's like you were a woman – let's say that bad girl Nunowna, and you showed me your thigh – Nunowna's thigh, that would be – and asked me: 'What shall I do with my thigh, it itches?' Is she as innocent as she pretends? Of course not. I catch a rabbit, but you catch a man. Man is made in God's image. Not so a rabbit, you know that. I'm a rabbit-eater, but you're a man-eater, Shauwa. And God will pass judgment on you. Shauwa, go home and repent. No, stop, there's something . . . [*He looks at the* OLD MAN *who stands trembling in the corner.*] No, it's nothing. Go home and repent. [*He slams the door behind* SHAUWA.] Now you're surprised, huh? Surprised I didn't hand you over? I couldn't hand over a bedbug to that animal. It goes against the grain. Now don't tremble because of a cop! So old and still so scared? Finish your cheese, but eat it like a poor man, or else they'll still catch you. Must I even explain how a poor man behaves? [*He pushes him down, and then gives him back the cheese.*] That box is the table. Lay your elbows on the table.

Now, encircle the cheese on the plate like it might be snatched from you at any moment – what right have you to be safe, huh? – now, hold your knife like an undersized sickle, and give your cheese a troubled look because, like all beautiful things, it's already fading away. [AZDAK *watches him.*] They're after you, which speaks in your favour, but how can we be sure they're not mistaken about you? In Tiflis one time they hanged a landowner, a Turk, who could prove he quartered his peasants instead of merely cutting them in half, as is the custom, and he squeezed twice the usual amount of taxes out of them, his zeal was above suspicion. And yet they hanged him like a common criminal – because he was a Turk – a thing he couldn't do much about. What injustice! He got onto the gallows by a sheer fluke. In short, I don't trust you.

THE SINGER:

Thus Azdak gave the old beggar a bed,

And learned that old beggar was the old butcher, the Grand Duke himself,

And was ashamed.

He denounced himself and ordered the policeman to take him to Nuka, to court, to be judged.

[*In the court of justice* THREE IRONSHIRTS *sit drinking. From a beam hangs a man in judge's robes. Enter* AZDAK, *in chains, dragging* SHAUWA *behind him*].

AZDAK [*shouting*]: I've helped the Grand Duke, the Grand Thief, the Grand Butcher, to escape! In the name of justice I ask to be severely judged in public trial!

THE FIRST IRONSHIRT: Who's this queer bird?

SHAUWA: That's our Village Scrivener, Azdak.

AZDAK: I am contemptible! I am a traitor! A branded criminal! Tell them, flatfoot, how I insisted on being tied up and brought to the capital. Because I sheltered the Grand Duke, the Grand Swindler, by mistake. And how I found out afterwards. See the marked man denounce himself! Tell them how I forced you to walk half the night with me to clear the whole thing up.

SHAUWA: And all by threats. That wasn't nice of you, Azdak.

AZDAK: Shut your mouth, Shauwa. You don't understand. A new age is upon us! It'll go thundering over you. You're finished. The police will be wiped out – poof! Everything will be gone into, everything will be brought into the open. The guilty will give themselves up. Why? They couldn't escape the people in any case. [*To* SHAUWA] Tell them how I shouted all along Shoemaker Street [*with big gestures, looking at the* IRONSHIRTS]: 'In my ignorance I let the Grand Swindler escape! So tear me to pieces, brothers!' I wanted to get it in first.

THE FIRST IRONSHIRT: And what did your brothers answer?

SHAUWA: They comforted him in Butcher Street, and they laughed themselves sick in Shoemaker Street. That's all.

AZDAK: But with you it's different. I can see you're men of iron. Brothers, where's the judge? I must be tried.

THE FIRST IRONSHIRT [*pointing at the hanged man*]: There's the judge. And please stop 'brothering' us. It's rather a sore spot this evening.

AZDAK: 'There's the judge.' An answer never heard in Grusinia before. Townsman, where's His Excellency the Governor? [*Pointing to the ground*] There's His Excellency, stranger. Where's the Chief Tax Collector? Where's the official Recruiting Officer? The Patriarch? The Chief of Police? There, there, there – all there. Brothers, I expected no less of you.

THE SECOND IRONSHIRT: What? *What* was it you expected, funny man?

AZDAK: What happened in Persia, brother, what happened in Persia?

THE SECOND IRONSHIRT: What did happen in Persia?

AZDAK: Everybody was hanged. Viziers, tax collectors. Everybody. Forty years ago now. My grandfather, a remarkable man by the way, saw it all. For three whole days. Everywhere.

THE SECOND IRONSHIRT: And who ruled when the Vizier was hanged?

AZDAK: A peasant rules when the Vizier was hanged.

THE SECOND IRONSHIRT: And who commanded the army?

AZDAK: A soldier, a soldier.

THE SECOND IRONSHIRT: And who paid the wages?

AZDAK: A dyer. A dyer paid the wages.

THE SECOND IRONSHIRT: Wasn't it a weaver, maybe?

THE FIRST IRONSHIRT: And why did all this happen, Persian?

AZDAK: Why did all this happen? Must there be a special reason? Why do you scratch yourself, brother? War! Too long a war! And no justice! My grandfather brought back a song that tells how it was. I will sing it for you. With my friend the policeman. [*To* SHAUWA] And hold the rope tight. It's very suitable. [*He sings,* with SHAUWA *holding the rope tight around him.*]

THE SONG OF INJUSTICE IN PERSIA

Why don't our sons bleed any more? Why don't our
daughters weep?
Why do only the slaughterhouse cattle have blood
in their veins?
Why do only the willows shed tears on Lake Urmia?
The king must have a new province, the peasant must
give up his savings.
That the roof of the world might be conquered, the
roof of the cottage is torn down.
Our men are carried to the ends of the earth, so
that great ones can eat at home.
The soldiers kill each other, the marshals salute each other.
They bite the widow's tax money to see if it's good,
their swords break.
The battle was lost, the helmets were paid for.

Refrain: Is it so? Is it so?

SHAUWA [*refrain*]: Yes, yes, yes, yes, yes it's so.

AZDAK: Want to hear the rest of it? [*The* FIRST IRONSHIRT *nods.*]

THE SECOND IRONSHIRT [*to* SHAUWA]: Did he teach you that song?

SHAUWA: Yes, only my voice isn't very good.

THE SECOND IRONSHIRT: No. [*To* AZDAK] Go on singing.

AZDAK: The second verse is about the peace. [*He sings.*]

> The offices are packed, the streets overflow with officials.
>
> The rivers jump their banks and ravage the fields.
>
> Those who cannot let down their own trousers rule countries.
>
> They can't count up to four, but they devour eight courses.
>
> The corn farmers, looking round for buyers, see only the starving.
>
> The weavers go home from their looms in rags.
>
> *Refrain*: Is it so? Is it so?

SHAUWA [*refrain*]: Yes, yes, yes, yes, yes it's so.

AZDAK:

> That's why our sons don't bleed any more, that's why our daughters don't weep.
>
> That's why only the slaughterhouse cattle have blood in their veins.
>
> And only the willows shed tears by Lake Urmia toward morning.

THE FIRST IRONSHIRT: Are you going to sing that song here in town?

AZDAK: Sure. What's wrong with it?

THE FIRST IRONSHIRT: Have you noticed that the sky's getting red? [*Turning round,* AZDAK *sees the sky red with fire.*] It's the people's quarters on the outskirts of town. The carpet weavers have caught the 'Persian Sickness', too. And they've been asking if Prince Kazbeki isn't eating too many courses. This morning they strung up the city judge. As for us we beat them to pulp. We were paid óne hundred piastres per man, you understand?

AZDAK [*after a pause*]: I understand. [*He glances shyly round and, creeping away, sits down in a corner, his head in his hands.*]

THE IRONSHIRTS [*to each other*]: If there ever was a trouble-maker it's him.

– He must've come to the capital to fish in the troubled waters.

SHAUWA: Oh, I don't think he's a really bad character, gentle-men. Steals a few chickens here and there. And maybe a rabbit.

THE SECOND IRONSHIRT [*approaching AZDAK*]: Came to fish in the troubled waters, huh?

AZDAK [*looking up*]: I don't know why I came.

THE SECOND IRONSHIRT: Are you in with the carpet weavers maybe? [AZDAK *shakes his head.*] How about that song?

AZDAK: From my grandfather. A silly and ignorant man.

THE SECOND IRONSHIRT: Right. And how about the dyer who paid the wages?

AZDAK [*muttering*]: That was in Persia.

THE FIRST IRONSHIRT: And this denouncing of yourself? Because you didn't hang the Grand Duke with your own hands?

AZDAK: Didn't I tell you I let him run? [*He creeps farther away and sits on the floor.*]

SHAUWA: I can swear to that: he let him run.

[*The* IRONSHIRTS *burst out laughing and slap* SHAUWA *on the back.* AZDAK *laughs loudest. They slap* AZDAK *too, and unchain him. They all start drinking as the* FAT PRINCE *enters with a* YOUNG MAN.]

THE FIRST IRONSHIRT [*to* AZDAK, *pointing at the* FAT PRINCE]: There's your 'new age' for you! [*More laughter.*]

THE FAT PRINCE: Well, my friends, what is there to laugh

about? Permit me a serious word. Yesterday morning the Princes of Grusinia overthrew the war-mongering government of the Grand Duke and did away with his Governors. Unfortunately the Grand Duke himself escaped. In this fateful hour our carpet weavers, those eternal troublemakers, had the effrontery to stir up a rebellion and hang the universally loved city judge, our dear Illo Orbeliani. Ts – ts – ts. My friends, we need peace, peace, peace in Grusinia! And justice! So I've brought along my dear nephew Bizergan Kazbeki. He'll be the new judge, hm? A very gifted fellow. What do you say? I want your opinion. Let the people decide!

THE SECOND IRONSHIRT: Does this mean *we* elect the judge?

THE FAT PRINCE: Precisely. Let the people propose some very gifted fellow! Confer among yourselves, my friends. [*The* IRONSHIRTS *confer.*] Don't worry, my little fox. The job's yours. And when we catch the Grand Duke we won't have to kiss this rabble's ass any longer.

THE IRONSHIRTS [*among themselves*]: Very funny: they're wetting their pants because they haven't caught the Grand Duke. – When the outlook isn't so bright, they say: 'My friends!' and 'Let the people decide!' – Now he even wants justice for Grusinia! But fun is fun as long as it lasts! [*Pointing at* AZDAK] *He* knows all about justice. Hey rascal, would you like this nephew fellow to be the judge?

AZDAK: Are you asking me? You're not asking *me*?!

THE FIRST IRONSHIRT: Why not? Anything for a laugh!

AZDAK: You'd like to test him to the marrow, correct? Have you a criminal on hand? An experienced one? So the candidate can show what he knows?

THE SECOND IRONSHIRT: Let's see. We do have a couple of doctors downstairs. Let's use them.

AZDAK: Oh, no, that's no good, we can't take real criminals till we're sure the judge will be appointed. He may be dumb, but he must be appointed, or the law is violated. And the law is a sensitive organ. It's like the spleen, you mustn't hit it – that would be fatal. Of course you can hang those two without violating the law, because there was no judge in the vicinity. But judgment, when pronounced, must be pronounced with absolute gravity – it's all such nonsense. Suppose, for instance, a judge jails a woman – let's say she's stolen a corn cake to feed her child – and this judge isn't wearing his robes – or maybe he's scratching himself while passing sentence and half his body is uncovered – a man's thigh *will* itch once in a while – the sentence this judge passes is a disgrace and the law is violated. In short it would be easier for a judge's robe and a judge's hat to pass judgment than for a man with no robe and no hat. If you don't treat it with respect, the law just disappears on you. Now you don't try out a bottle of wine by offering it to a dog: you'd only lose your wine.

THE FIRST IRONSHIRT: Then what do you suggest, hairsplitter?

AZDAK: I'll be the defendant.

THE FIRST IRONSHIRT: You? [*He bursts out laughing.*]

THE FAT PRINCE: What have you decided?

THE FIRST IRONSHIRT: We've decided to stage a rehearsal. Our friend here will be the defendant. Let the candidate be the judge and sit there.

THE FAT PRINCE: It isn't customary, but why not? [*To the* NEPHEW] A mere formality, my little fox. What have I taught you? Who got there first – the slow runner or the fast?

THE NEPHEW: The silent runner, Uncle Arsen.

[*The* NEPHEW *takes the chair. The* IRONSHIRTS *and the* FAT PRINCE *sit on the steps. Enter* AZDAK, *mimicking the gait of the Grand Duke.*]

AZDAK [*in the Grand Duke's accent*]: Is any here knows me? Am Grand Duke.

THE IRONSHIRTS: *What* is he?
- The Grand Duke. He knows him too.
- Fine. So get on with the trial.
AZDAK: Listen! Am accused instigating war? Ridiculous! Am saying ridiculous! That enough? If not, have brought lawyers. Believe five hundred. [*He points behind him, pretending to be surrounded by lawyers.*] Requisition all available seats for lawyers!

[*The* IRONSHIRTS *laugh; the* FAT PRINCE *joins in.*]

THE NEPHEW [*to the* IRONSHIRTS]: You really wish me to try this case? I find it rather unusual. From the taste angle I mean.
THE FIRST IRONSHIRT: Let's go!
THE FAT PRINCE [*smiling*]: Let him have it, my little fox!
THE NEPHEW: All right. People of Grusinia versus Grand Duke. Defendant, what have you got to say for your self?
AZDAK: Plenty. Naturally, have read war lost. Only started on the advice of patriots. Like Uncle Arsen Kazbeki. Call Uncle Arsen as witness.
THE FAT PRINCE [*to the* IRONSHIRTS, *delightedly*]: What a screwball!
THE NEPHEW: Motion rejected. One cannot be arraigned for declaring a war, which every ruler has to do once in a while, but only for running a war badly.
AZDAK: Rubbish! Did not run it at all! Had it run! Had it run by Princes! Naturally, they messed it up.
THE NEPHEW: Do you by any chance deny having been commander-in-chief?
AZDAK: Not at all! Always *was* commander-in-chief. At birth shouted at wet nurse. Was trained drop turds in toilet, grew accustomed to command. Always commanded officials rob my cash box. Officers flog soldiers only on command. Landowners sleep with peasants' wives only on strictest command. Uncle Arsen here grew his belly at *my* command!
THE IRONSHIRTS [*clapping*]: He's good! Long live the Grand Duke!

THE FAT PRINCE: Answer him, my little fox. I'm with you.

THE NEPHEW: I shall answer him according to the dignity of the law. Defendant, preserve the dignity of the law!

AZDAK: Agreed. Command you proceed with trial!

THE NEPHEW: It is not your place to command me. You claim that the Princes forced you to declare war. How can you claim, then, that they – er – 'messed it up'?

AZDAK: Did not send enough people. Embezzled funds. Sent sick horses. During attack, drinking in whore-house. Call Uncle Arsen as witness.

THE NEPHEW: Are you making the outrageous suggestion that the Princes of this country did not fight?

AZDAK: No. Princes fought. Fought for war contracts.

THE FAT PRINCE [jumping up]: That's too much! This man talks like a carpet weaver!

AZDAK: Really? Told nothing but truth.

THE FAT PRINCE: Hang him! Hang him!

THE FIRST IRONSHIRT [pulling the PRINCE down]: Keep quiet! Go on Excellency!

THE NEPHEW: Quiet! I now render a verdict: You must be hanged! By the neck! Having lost war!

AZDAK: Young man, seriously advise not fall publicly into jerky clipped speech. Cannot be watchdog if howl like wolf. Got it? If people realize Princes speak same language as Grand Duke, may hang Grand Duke and Princes, huh? By the way, must overrule verdict. Reason? War lost, but not for Princes. Princes won their war. Got 3,863,000 piastres for horses not delivered, 8,240,000 piastres for food supplies not produced. Are therefore victors. War lost only for Grusinia, which is not present in this court.

THE FAT PRINCE: I think that will do, my friends. [To AZDAK] You can withdraw, funny man. [To the IRONSHIRTS] You may now ratify the new judge's appointment, my friends.

THE FIRST IRONSHIRT: Yes, we can. Take down the judge's gown. [ONE IRONSHIRT climbs on the back of the OTHER,

pulls the gown off the hanged man.] [*To the* NEPHEW] Now
you run away so the right ass can get on the right chair. [*To*
AZDAK] Step forward! Go to the judge's seat! Now sit in it!
[AZDAK *steps up, bows, and sits down.*] The judge was always a
rascal! Now the rascal shall be a judge! [*The judge's gown is
placed round his shoulders, the hat on his head.*] And what a
judge!

THE SINGER:

And there was civil war in the land.
The mighty were not safe.
And Azdak was made a judge by the Ironshirts.
And Azdak remained a judge for two years.

THE SINGER AND CHORUS:

When the towns were set afire
And rivers of blood rose higher and higher,
Cockroaches crawled out of every crack.
And the court was full of schemers
And the church of foul blasphemers.
In the judge's cassock sat Azdak.

[AZDAK *sits in the judge's chair, peeling an apple.* SHAUWA
is sweeping out the hall. On one side an INVALID *in a wheel-
chair. Opposite, a* YOUNG MAN *accused of blackmail. An*
IRONSHIRT *stands guard, holding the Ironshirts' banner.*]

AZDAK: In consideration of the large number of cases, the
Court today will hear two cases at a time. Before I open the
proceedings, a short announcement – I accept. [*He stretches
out his hand. The* BLACKMAILER *is the only one to produce any
money. He hands it to* AZDAK.] I reserve the right to punish
one of the parties for contempt of court. [*He glances at the
INVALID.*] You [*to the* DOCTOR] are a doctor, and you [*to the*
INVALID] are bringing a complaint against him. Is the doctor responsible for your condition?

THE INVALID: Yes. I had a stroke on his account.

AZDAK: That would be professional negligence.

THE INVALID: Worse than negligence. I gave this man money

for his studies. So far, he hasn't paid me back a cent. It was when I heard he was treating a patient free that I had my stroke.

AZDAK: Rightly. [*To a* LIMPING MAN] And what are *you* doing here?

THE LIMPING MAN: I'm the patient, Your Honour.

AZDAK: He treated your leg for nothing?

THE LIMPING MAN: The wrong leg! My rheumatism was in the left leg, he operated on the right. That's why I limp.

AZDAK: And you were treated free?

THE INVALID: A five-hundred-piastre operation free! For nothing! For a God-bless-you! And I paid for this man's studies! [*To the* DOCTOR] Did they teach you to operate free?

THE DOCTOR: Your Honour, it is the custom to demand the fee before the operation, as the patient is more willing to pay before an operation than after. Which is only human. In the case in question I was convinced, when I started the operation, that my servant had already received the fee. In this I was mistaken.

THE INVALID: He was mistaken! A good doctor doesn't make mistakes! He examines before he operates!

AZDAK: That's right. [*To* SHAUWA] Public Prosecutor, what's the other case about?

SHAUWA [*busily sweeping*]: Blackmail.

THE BLACKMAILER: High Court of Justice, I'm innocent. I only wanted to find out from the landowner concerned if he really *had* raped his niece. He informed me very politely that this was not the case, and gave me the money only so I could pay for my uncle's studies.

AZDAK: Hm. [*To the* DOCTOR] You, on the other hand, can cite no extenuating circumstances for your offence, huh?

THE DOCTOR: Except that to err is human.

AZDAK: And you are aware that in money matters a good doctor is a highly responsible person? I once heard of a doctor who got a thousand piastres for a sprained finger by remarking that sprains have something to do with blood circulation, which after all a less good doctor might have overlooked, and who, on another occasion made a real gold mine out of a somewhat disordered gallbladder, he treated it with such loving care. You have no excuse, Doctor. The corn merchant Uxu had his son study medicine to get some knowledge of trade, our medical schools are so good. [*To the* BLACKMAILER] What's the landowner's name?

SHAUWA: He doesn't want it mentioned.

AZDAK: In that case I will pass judgment. The Court considers the blackmail proved. And you [*to the* INVALID] are sentenced to a fine of one thousand piastres. If you have a second stroke, the doctor will have to treat you free. Even if he has to amputate. [*To the* LIMPING MAN] As compensation, you will receive a bottle of rubbing alcohol. [*To the* BLACKMAILER] You are sentenced to hand over half the proceeds of your deal to the Public Prosecutor to keep the landowner's name secret. You are advised, moreover, to study medicine – you seem well suited to that calling. [*To the* DOCTOR] You have perpetrated an unpardonable error in the practice of your profession: you are acquitted. Next cases!

THE SINGER AND CHORUS:
Men won't do much for a shilling.
For a pound they may be willing.
For twenty pounds the verdict's in the sack.
As for the many, all too many,
Those who've only got a penny –
They've one single, sole recourse: Azdak.

[*Enter* AZDAK *from the caravansary on the high road, followed by an old bearded* INNKEEPER. *The judge's chair is carried by a* STABLEMAN *and* SHAUWA. *An* IRONSHIRT, *with a banner, takes up his position.*]

AZDAK: Put me down. Then we'll get some air, maybe even a good stiff breeze from the lemon grove there. It does justice good to be done in the open: the wind blows her skirts up and you can see what she's got. Shauwa, we've been eating too much. These official journeys are exhausting. [*To the* INNKEEPER] It's a question of your daughter-in-law?

THE INNKEEPER: Your Worship, it's a question of the family honour. I wish to bring an action on behalf of my son, who's away on business on the other side the mountain. This is the offending stableman, and here's my daughter-in-law.

[*Enter the* DAUGHTER-IN-LAW, *a voluptuous wench. She is veiled.*]

AZDAK [*sitting down*]: I accept. [*Sighing the* INNKEEPER *hands him some money.*] Good. Now the formalities are disposed of. This is a case of rape?

THE INNKEEPER: Your Honour, I caught the fellow in the act. Ludovica was in the straw on the stable floor.

AZDAK: Quite right, the stable. Lovely horses! I specially liked the little roan.

THE INNKEEPER: The first thing I did, of course, was to question Ludovica. On my son's behalf.

AZDAK [*seriously*]: I said I specially liked the little roan.

THE INNKEEPER [*coldly*]: Really? Ludovica confessed the stableman took her against her will.

AZDAK: Take your veil off, Ludovica. [*She does so.*] Ludovica, you please the Court. Tell us how it happened.

LUDOVICA [*well schooled*]: When I entered the stable to see the new foal the stableman said to me on his own accord: 'It's hot today!' and laid his hand on my left breast. I said to him: 'Don't do that!' But he continued to handle me indecently, which provoked my anger. Before I realized his sinful intentions, he got much closer. It was all over when my father-in-law entered and accidentally trod on me.

THE INNKEEPER [*explaining*]: On my son's behalf.

AZDAK [*to the* STABLEMAN]: You admit you started it?

THE STABLEMAN: Yes.

AZDAK: Ludovica, you like to eat sweet things?

LUDOVICA: Yes, sunflower seeds!

AZDAK: You like to lie a long time in the bathtub?

LUDOVICA: Half an hour or so.

AZDAK: Public Prosecutor, drop your knife – there – on the ground. [SHAUWA *does so*.] Ludovica, pick up that knife. [LUDOVICA, *swaying her hips, does so*.] See that? [*He points at her*.] The way it moves? The rape is now proven. By eating too much – sweet things, especially – by lying too long in warm water, by laziness and too soft a skin, you have raped that unfortunate man. Think you can run around with a behind like that and get away with it in court? This is a case of intentional assault with a dangerous weapon! You are sentenced to hand over to the Court the little roan which your father liked to ride 'on his son's behalf'. And now, come with me to the stables, so the Court can inspect the scene of the crime, Ludovica.

THE SINGER AND CHORUS:
When the sharks the sharks devour
Little fishes have their hour.
For a while the load is off their back.
On Grusinia's highways faring
Fixed-up scales of justice bearing
Strode the poor man's magistrate: Azdak.

And he gave to the forsaken
All that from the rich he'd taken.
And a body-guard of roughnecks was Azdak's.
And our good and evil man, he
Smiled upon Grusinia's Granny.
His emblem was a tear in sealing wax.

All mankind should love each other
But when visiting your brother
Take an axe along and hold it fast.
Not in theory but in practice.
Miracles are wrought with axes
And the age of miracles is not past.

[AZDAK'S *judge's chair is in a tavern.* THREE RICH FARM-
ERS *stand before* AZDAK. SHAUWA *brings him wine. In a
corner stands an* OLD PEASANT WOMAN. *In the open doorway, and outside, stand* VILLAGERS *looking on. An* IRON-
SHIRT *stands guard with a banner.*]

AZDAK: The Public Prosecutor has the floor.

SHAUWA: It concerns a cow. For five weeks the defendant has
had a cow in her stable, the property of the farmer Suru.
She was also found to be in possession of a stolen ham,
and a number of cows belonging to Shutoff were killed
after he asked the defendant to pay the rent on a piece of
land.

THE FARMERS: It's a matter of my ham, Your Honour.
  – It's a matter of my cow, Your Honour.
  – It's a matter of my land, Your Honour.

AZDAK: Well, Granny, what have *you* got to say to all this?

THE OLD WOMAN: Your Honour, one night toward morning,
five weeks ago, there was a knock at my door, and outside
stood a bearded man with a cow. 'My dear woman,' he
said, 'I am the miracle-working Saint Banditus and because
your son has been killed in the war, I bring you this cow as a
souvenir. Take good care of it.'

THE FARMERS: The robber, Irakli, Your Honour!
  – Her brother-in-law, Your Honour!
  – The cow-thief!
  – The incendiary!
  – He must be beheaded!
    [*Outside, a woman screams. The* CROWD *grows restless, re-
    treats. Enter the* BANDIT IRAKLI *with a huge axe.*]

THE BANDIT: A very good evening, dear friends! A glass of
vodka!

THE FARMERS [*crossing themselves*]: Irakli!

AZDAK: Public Prosecutor, a glass of vodka for our guest. And
who are you?

THE BANDIT: I'm a wandering hermit, Your Honour. Thanks

for the gracious gift. [*He empties the glass which* SHAUWA *has brought.*] Another!

AZDAK: I am Azdak. [*He gets up and bows. The* BANDIT *also bows.*] The Court welcomes the foreign hermit. Go on with your story, Granny.

THE OLD WOMAN: Your Honour, that first night I didn't yet know Saint Banditus could work miracles, it was only the cow. But one night, a few days later, the farmer's servants came to take the cow away again. Then they turned round in front of my door and went off without the cow. And bumps as big as a fist sprouted on their heads. So I knew that Saint Banditus had changed their hearts and turned them into friendly people.

[*The* BANDIT *roars with laughter.*]

THE FIRST FARMER: I know what changed them.

AZDAK: That's fine. You can tell us later. Continue.

THE OLD WOMAN: Your Honour, the next one to become a good man was the farmer Shutoff – a devil, as everyone knows. But Saint Banditus arranged it so he let me off the rent on the little piece of land.

THE SECOND FARMER: Because my cows were killed in the fields.

[*The* BANDIT *laughs.*]

THE OLD WOMAN [*answering* AZDAK'S *sign to continue*]: Then one morning the ham came flying in at my window. It hit me in the small of the back. I'm still lame, Your Honour, look. [*She limps a few steps. The* BANDIT *laughs.*] Your Honour, was there ever a time when a poor old woman could get a ham *without* a miracle?

[*The* BANDIT *starts sobbing.*]

AZDAK [*rising from his chair*]: Granny, that's a question that strikes straight at the Court's heart. Be so kind as to sit here.

[*The* OLD WOMAN, *hesitating, sits in the judge's chair.*]

AZDAK [*sits on the floor, glass in hand, reciting*]:

Granny
We could almost call you Granny Grusinia
The Woebegone
The Bereaved Mother
Whose sons have gone to war
Receiving the present of a cow
She bursts out crying.
When she is beaten
She remains hopeful.
When she's not beaten
She's surprised.
On us
Who are already damned
May you render a merciful verdict
Granny Grusinia!

[*Bellowing at the* FARMERS] Admit you don't believe in miracles, you atheists! Each of you is sentenced to pay five hundred piastres! For godlessness! Get out! [*The* FARMERS *slink out.*] And you Granny, and you [*to the* BANDIT] pious man, empty a pitcher of wine with the Public Prosecutor and Azdak!

THE SINGER AND CHORUS:
And he broke the rules to save them.
Broken law like bread he gave them,
Brought them to shore upon his crooked back.
At long last the poor and lowly
Had someone who was not too holy
To be bribed by empty hands: Azdak.

For two years it was his pleasure
To give the beast of prey short measure:
He became a wolf to fight the pack.
From All Hallows to All Hallows
On his chair beside the gallows
Dispensing justice in his fashion sat Azdak.

THE SINGER:
　But the era of disorder came to an end.
　The Grand Duke returned.
　The Governor's wife returned.
　A trial was held.
　Many died.
　The people's quarters burned anew.
　And fear seized Azdak.

　　[AZDAK's *judge's chair stands again in the court of justice.* AZDAK *sits on the floor, shaving and talking to* SHAUWA. *Noises outside. In the rear the* FAT PRINCE's *head is carried on a lance.*]

AZDAK: Shauwa, the days of your slavery are numbered, maybe even the minutes. For a long time now I have held you in the iron curb of reason, and it has torn your mouth till it bleeds. I have lashed you with reasonable arguments, I have manhandled you with logic. You are by nature a weak man, and if one slyly throws an argument in your path, you *have* to snap it up, you can't resist. It is your nature to lick the hand of some superior being. But superior beings can be of very different kinds. And now, with your liberation, you will soon be able to follow your natural inclinations, which are low. You will be able to follow your infallible instinct, which teaches you to plant your fat heel on the faces of men. Gone is the era of confusion and disorder, which I find described in the Song of Chaos. Let us now sing that song together in memory of those terrible days. Sit down and don't do violence to the music. Don't be afraid. It sounds all right. And it has a fine refrain. [*He sings.*]

THE SONG OF CHAOS

Sister, hide your face! Brother, take your knife!
The times are out of joint!
Big men are full of complaint
And small men full of joy.

The city says:
'Let us drive the mighty from our midst!'
Offices are raided. Lists of serfs are destroyed.
They have set Master's nose to the grindstone.
They who lived in the dark have come out into the light.
The ebony poor boxes are smashed to bits.
Sesnem* wood is sawed up for beds.
Who had no bread have granaries.
Who begged for corn now mete it out.
SHAUWA [refrain]: Oh, oh, oh, oh.
AZDAK [refrain]:
Where are you, General, where are you?
Please, please, please, restore order!

The nobleman's son can no longer be recognized;
The lady's child becomes the son of her slave.
The people's councils meet in a barn.
Once, this man was barely allowed to sleep on the wall;
Now, he stretches his limbs in a bed.
Once, this man rowed a boat; now, he owns ships.
Their owner looks for them, but they're his no longer.
Five men are sent on a journey by their master.
'Go yourself,' they say, 'we have arrived.'
SHAUWA [refrain]: Oh, oh, oh, oh.
AZDAK [refrain]:
Where are you, General, where are you?
Please, please, please, restore order!

* I do not know what kind of wood this is, so I have left the word exactly as it stands in the German original. The song is based on an Egyptian papyrus which Brecht cites as such in his essay, 'Five Difficulties in the Writing of the Truth'. I should think he must have come across it in Adolf Erman's Die Literatur der Aegypter, 1923, pp. 130 ff. Erman too gives the word as Sesnem. The same papyrus is quoted in Karl Jaspers' Man in the Modern Age (Routledge, 1951) but without the sentence about the Sesnem wood.   E.B.

Yes, so it might have been, had order been neglected much longer. But now the Grand Duke has returned to the capital, and the Persians have lent him an army to restore order with. The people's quarters are already aflame. Go and get me the big book I always sit on. [SHAUWA *brings the big book from the judge's chair.* AZDAK *opens it.*] This is the Statute Book and I've always used it, as you can testify. Now I'd better look in this book and see what they can do to me. I've let the down-and-outs get away with murder, and I'll have to pay for it. I helped poverty onto its skinny legs, so they'll hang me for drunkenness. I peeped into the rich man's pocket, which is bad taste. And I can't hide anywhere – everybody knows me because I've helped everybody.

SHAUWA: Someone's coming!

AZDAK [*in panic, he walks trembling to the chair*]: It's the end. And now they'd enjoy seeing what a Great Man I am. I'll deprive them of that pleasure. I'll beg on my knees for mercy. Spittle will slobber down my chin. The fear of death is in me.

[*Enter Natella Abashwili, the* GOVERNOR'S WIFE, *followed by the* ADJUTANT *and an* IRONSHIRT.]

THE GOVERNOR'S WIFE: What sort of a creature is that, Shalva?

AZDAK: A willing one, Your Highness, a man ready to oblige.

THE ADJUTANT: Natella Abashwili, wife of the late Governor, has just returned. She is looking for her two-year-old son, Michael. She has been informed that the child was carried off to the mountains by a former servant.

AZDAK: The child will be brought back, Your Highness, at your service.

THE ADJUTANT: They say that the person in question is passing it off as her own.

AZDAK: She will be beheaded, Your Highness, at your service.

THE ADJUTANT: That is all.

THE GOVERNOR'S WIFE [*leaving*]: I don't like that man.

AZDAK [*following her to door, bowing*]: At your service, Your Highness, it will all be arranged.

5. The Chalk Circle

THE SINGER:

Hear now the story of the trial
Concerning Governor Abashwili's child
And the determination of the true mother
By the famous test of the Chalk Circle.

[*Law court in Nuka.* IRONSHIRTS *lead* MICHAEL *across stage and out at the back.* IRONSHIRTS *hold* GRUSHA *back with their lances under the gateway until the* CHILD *has been led through. Then she is admitted. She is accompanied by the former Governor's* COOK. *Distant noises and a fire-red sky.*]

GRUSHA [*trying to hide*]: He's brave, he can wash himself now.

THE COOK: You're lucky. It's not a real judge. It's Azdak, a drunk who doesn't know what he's doing. The biggest thieves have got by through him. Because he gets everything mixed up and the rich never offer him big enough bribes, the likes of us sometimes do pretty well.

GRUSHA: I need luck right now.

THE COOK: Touch wood. [*She crosses herself.*] I'd better offer up another prayer that the judge may be drunk. [*She prays with motionless lips, while* GRUSHA *looks around, in vain, for the child.*] Why must you hold on to it at any price if it isn't yours? In days like these?

GRUSHA: He's mine. I brought him up.

THE COOK: Have you never thought what'd happen when she came back?

GRUSHA: At first I thought I'd give him to her. Then I thought she wouldn't come back.

THE COOK: And even a borrowed coat keeps a man warm,

hm? [GRUSHA *nods.*] I'll swear to anything for you. You're
a decent girl. [*She sees the soldier* SIMON SHASHAVA *approaching.*] You've done wrong by Simon, though. I've
been talking with him. He just can't understand.

GRUSHA [*unaware of* SIMON'S *presence*]: Right now I can't be
bothered whether he understands or not!

THE COOK: He knows the child isn't yours, but you married
and not free 'till death you do part' – he can't understand
that.

[GRUSHA *sees* SIMON *and greets him.*]

SIMON [*gloomily*]: I wish the lady to know I will swear I am
the father of the child.

GRUSHA [*low*]: Thank you, Simon.

SIMON: At the same time I wish the lady to know my hands
are not tied – nor are hers.

THE COOK: You needn't have said that. You know she's married.

SIMON: And it needs no rubbing in.

[*Enter an* IRONSHIRT.]

THE IRONSHIRT: Where's the judge? Has anyone seen the
judge?

ANOTHER IRONSHIRT [*stepping forward*]: The judge isn't here
yet. Nothing but a bed and a pitcher in the whole house!

[*Exeunt* IRONSHIRTS.]

THE COOK: I hope nothing has happened to him. With any
other judge you'd have as much chance as a chicken has
teeth.

GRUSHA [*who has turned away and covered her face*]: Stand in
front of me. I shouldn't have come to Nuka. If I run into the
Ironshirt, the one I hit over the head . . . [*She screams.*]

[*An* IRONSHIRT *had stopped and, turning his back, has been
listening to her. He now wheels around. It is the* CORPORAL
and he has a huge scar across his face.]

THE IRONSHIRT [*in the gateway*]: What's the matter, Shotta?
Do you know her?

THE CORPORAL [*after staring for some time*]: No.

THE IRONSHIRT: She's the one who stole the Abashwili child, or so they say. If you know anything about it you can make some money, Shotta.

[*Exit the* CORPORAL, *cursing.*]

THE COOK: Was it him? [GRUSHA *nods.*] I think he'll keep his mouth shut, or he'd be admitting he was after the child.

GRUSHA: I'd almost forgotten him.

[*Enter the* GOVERNOR'S WIFE, *followed by the* ADJUTANT *and* TWO LAWYERS.]

THE GOVERNOR'S WIFE: At least there are no common people here, thank God. I can't stand their smell. It always gives me migraine.

THE FIRST LAWYER: Madam, I must ask you to be careful what you say until we have another judge.

THE GOVERNOR'S WIFE: But I didn't say anything, Illo Shuboladze. I love the people with their simple straightforward minds. It's only that their smell brings on my migraine.

THE SECOND LAWYER: There won't be many spectators. The whole population is sitting at home behind locked doors because of the riots in the people's quarters.

THE GOVERNOR'S WIFE [*looking at* GRUSHA]: Is that the creature?

THE FIRST LAWYER: Please, most gracious Natella Abashwili, abstain from invective until it is certain the Grand Duke has appointed a new judge and we're rid of the present one, who's about the lowest fellow ever seen in judge's gown. Things are all set to move, you see.

[*Enter* IRONSHIRTS *from the courtyard.*]

THE COOK: Her Grace would pull your hair out on the spot if she didn't know Azdak is for the poor. He goes by the face.

[IRONSHIRTS *begin fastening a rope to a beam.* AZDAK, *in chains, is led in, followed by* SHAUWA, *also in chains. The* THREE FARMERS *bring up the rear.*]

AN IRONSHIRT: Trying to run away, were you? [*He strikes* AZDAK.]

ONE FARMER: Off with his judge's gown before we string him up!

[IRONSHIRTS *and* FARMERS *tear off* AZDAK'S *gown. His torn underwear is visible. Then someone kicks him.*]

AN IRONSHIRT [*pushing him into someone else*]: Want a load of justice? Here it is! [*Accompanied by shouts of* 'You take it!' *and* 'Let me have him, Brother!' *they throw* AZDAK *back and forth until he collapses. Then he is lifted up and dragged under the noose.*]

THE GOVERNOR'S WIFE [*who, during this 'ballgame', has clapped her hands hysterically*]: I disliked that man from the moment I first saw him.

AZDAK [*covered with blood, panting*]: I can't see. Give me a rag.

AN IRONSHIRT: What is it you want to see?

AZDAK: You, you dogs! [*He wipes the blood out of his eyes with his shirt.*] Good morning, dogs! How goes it, dogs! How's the dog world? Does it smell good? Got another boot for me to lick? Are you back at each other's throats, dogs?

[*Accompanied by a* CORPORAL, *a dust-covered* RIDER *enters. He takes some documents from a leather case, looks at them, then interrupts.*]

THE RIDER: Stop! I bring a dispatch from the Grand Duke, containing the latest appointments.

THE CORPORAL [*bellowing*]: Atten – shun!

THE RIDER: Of the new judge it says: 'We appoint a man whom we have to thank for saving a life indispensable to the country's welfare – a certain Azdak of Nuka.' Which is he?

SHAUWA [*pointing*]: That's him, Your Excellency.

THE CORPORAL [*bellowing*]: What's going on here?

AN IRONSHIRT: I beg to report that His Honour Azdak was already His Honour Azdak, but on these farmers' denunciation was pronounced the Grand Duke's enemy.

THE CORPORAL [*pointing at the* FARMERS]: March them off!

[*They are marched off. They bow all the time.*] See to it that His Honour Azdak is exposed to no more violence.

[*Exeunt* RIDER *and* CORPORAL.]

THE COOK [*to* SHAUWA]: She clapped her hands! I hope he saw it!

THE FIRST LAWYER: It's a catastrophe.

[AZDAK *has fainted. Coming to, he is dressed again in judge's robes. He walks, swaying, toward the* IRONSHIRTS.]

AN IRONSHIRT: What does Your Honour desire?

AZDAK: Nothing, fellow dogs, or just an occasional boot to lick. [*To* SHAUWA] I pardon you. [*He is unchained.*] Get me some red wine, the sweet kind. [SHAUWA *stumbles off.*] Get out of here, I've got to judge a case. [*Exeunt* IRONSHIRTS. SHAUWA *returns with a pitcher of wine.* AZDAK *gulps it down.*] Something for my backside. [SHAUWA *brings the Statute Book, puts it on the judge's chair,* AZDAK *sits on it.*] I accept.

[*The* PROSECUTORS, *among whom a worried council has been held, smile with relief. They whisper.*]

THE COOK: Oh dear!

SIMON: A well can't be filled with dew, they say.

THE LAWYERS [*approaching* AZDAK, *who stands up, expectantly*]: A quite ridiculous case, Your Honour. The accused has abducted a child and refuses to hand it over.

AZDAK [*stretching out his hand, glancing at* GRUSHA]: A most attractive person. [*He fingers the money, then sits down, satisfied.*] I declare the proceedings open and demand the whole truth. [*To* GRUSHA] Especially from you.

THE FIRST LAWYER: High Court of Justice! Blood, as the popular saying goes, is thicker than water. This old adage . . .

AZDAK [*interrupting*]: The Court wants to know the lawyers' fee.

THE FIRST LAWYER [*surprised*]: I beg your pardon? [AZDAK, *smiling, rubs his thumb and index finger.*] Oh, I see. Five hundred piastres, Your Honour, to answer the Court's somewhat unusual question.

GIBERT JEUNE
VOUS REMERCIE

14 MAR '79

· · · · · 5 NK · · · · 48.50 *

· 110 E· · · · · · 48.50 CT

The question is unusual. I ask it because
[dif]ferent way when I know you're good.
[bowing]: Thank you, Your Honour.
[...], of all ties the ties of blood are strong-
[...] – is there a more intimate relationship?
[...]om its mother? High Court of Justice,
[...]in the holy ecstasies of love. She has
[...]b. She has fed it with her blood. She
[...]n. High Court of Justice, it has been
[...]e wild tigress, robbed of her young,
[...] the mountains, shrunk to a shadow.
Nature herself . . .

AZDAK [interrupting, to GRUSHA]: What's your answer to all
this and anything else that lawyer might have to say?

GRUSHA: He's mine.

AZDAK: Is that all? I hope you can prove it. Why should I assign
the child to you in any case?

GRUSHA: I brought him up like the priest says 'according to
my best knowledge and conscience'. I always found him
something to eat. Most of the time he had a roof over his
head. And I went to such trouble for him. I had expenses
too. I didn't look out for my own comfort. I brought the
child up to be friendly with everyone, and from the beginning taught him to work. As well as he could, that is. He's
still very little.

THE FIRST LAWYER: Your Honour, it is significant that the
girl herself doesn't claim any tie of blood between her and
the child.

AZDAK: The Court takes note of that.

THE FIRST LAWYER: Thank you, Your Honour. And now
permit a woman bowed in sorrow – who has already lost
her husband and now has also to fear the loss of her child –
to address a few words to you. The gracious Natella Abashwili is . . .

THE GOVERNOR'S WIFE [quietly]: A most cruel fate, sir, forces

me to describe to you the tortures of a bereaved mother's
soul, the anxiety, the sleepless nights, the . . .

THE SECOND LAWYER [bursting out]: It's outrageous the way
this woman is being treated! Her husband's palace is closed
to her! The revenue of her estates is blocked, and she is
cold-bloodedly told that it's tied to the heir. She can't do a
thing without that child. She can't even pay her lawyers! !
[To the FIRST LAWYER, who, desperate about this outburst,
makes frantic gestures to keep him from speaking] Dear Illo Shuboladze, surely it can be divulged now that the Abashwili
estates are at stake?

THE FIRST LAWYER: Please, Honoured Sandro Oboladze! We
agreed . . . [To AZDAK] Of course it is correct that the trial
will also decide if our noble client can dispose of the Abashwili estates, which are rather extensive. I say 'also' advisedly,
for in the foreground stands the human tragedy of a mother,
as Natella Abashwili very properly explained in the first
words of her moving statement. Even if Michael Abashwili
were not heir to the estates, he would still be the dearly beloved child of my client.

AZDAK: Stop! The Court is touched by the mention of estates.
It's a proof of human feeling.

THE SECOND LAWYER: Thanks, Your Honour. Dear Illo Shuboladze, we can prove in any case that the woman who took
the child is not the child's mother. Permit me to lay before
the Court the bare facts. High Court of Justice, by an unfortunate chain of circumstances, Michael Abashwili was
left behind on that Easter Sunday while his mother was
making her escape. Grusha, a palace kitchen maid, was seen
with the baby . . .

THE COOK: All her mistress was thinking of was what dresses
she'd take along!

THE SECOND LAWYER [unmoved]: Nearly a year later Grusha
turned up in a mountain village with a baby and there entered into the state of matrimony with . . .

AZDAK: How'd you get to that mountain village?

GRUSHA: On foot, Your Honour. And he was mine.

SIMON: I'm the father, Your Honour.

THE COOK: I used to look after it for them, Your Honour. For five piastres.

THE SECOND LAWYER: This man is engaged to Grusha, High Court of Justice: his testimony is suspect.

AZDAK: Are you the man she married in the mountain village?

SIMON: No, Your Honour, she married a peasant.

AZDAK [to GRUSHA]: Why? [Pointing at SIMON] Is he no good in bed? Tell the truth.

GRUSHA: We didn't get that far. I married because of the baby. So he'd have a roof over his head. [Pointing at SIMON] He was in the war, Your Honour.

AZDAK: And now he wants you back again, huh?

SIMON: I wish to state in evidence . . .

GRUSHA [angrily]: I am no longer free, Your Honour.

AZDAK: And the child, you claim, comes from whoring? [GRUSHA doesn't answer.] I'm going to ask you a question: What kind of child is he? A ragged little bastard? Or from a good family?

GRUSHA [angrily]: He's an ordinary child.

AZDAK: I mean – did he have refined features from the beginning?

GRUSHA: He had a nose on his face.

AZDAK: A very significant comment! It has been said of me that I went out one time and sniffed at a rosebud before rendering a verdict – tricks like that are needed nowadays. Well, I'll make it short, and not listen to any more lies. [To GRUSHA] Especially not yours. [To all the accused] I can imagine what you've cooked up to cheat me! I know you people. You're swindlers.

GRUSHA [suddenly]: I can understand your wanting to cut it short, now I've seen what you accepted!

AZDAK: Shut up! Did I accept anything from you?

GRUSHA [*while the* COOK *tries to restrain her*]: I haven't got any-thing.

AZDAK: True. Quite true. From starvelings I never get a thing. I might just as well starve, myself. You want justice, but do you want to pay for it, hm? When you go to a butcher you know you have to pay, but you people go to a judge as if you were off to a funeral supper.

SIMON [*loudly*]: When the horse was shod, the horsefly held out its leg, as the saying is.

AZDAK [*eagerly accepting the challenge*]: Better a treasure in manure than a stone in a mountain stream.

SIMON: A fine day. Let's go fishing, said the angler to the worm.

AZDAK: I'm my own master, said the servant, and cut off his foot.

SIMON: I love you as a father, said the Tsar to the peasants, and had the Tsarevitch's head chopped off.

AZDAK: A fool's worst enemy is himself.

SIMON: However, a fart has no nose.

AZDAK: Fined ten piastres for indecent language in court! That'll teach you what justice is.

GRUSHA [*furiously*]: A fine kind of justice! You play fast and loose with us because we don't talk as refined as that crowd with their lawyers!

AZDAK: That's true. You people are too dumb. It's only right you should get it in the neck.

GRUSHA: You want to hand the child over to her, and she wouldn't even know how to keep it dry, she's so 'refined'! You know about as much about justice as I do!

AZDAK: There's something in that. I'm an ignorant man. Haven't even a decent pair of pants on under this gown. Look! With me, everything goes on food and drink – I was educated in a convent. Incidentally, I'll fine you ten piastres for contempt of court. And you're a very silly girl, to turn me against you, instead of making eyes at me and wiggling your backside a little to keep me in a good temper. Twenty piastres!

GRUSHA: Even if it was thirty, I'd tell you what I think of your justice, you drunken onion! [*Incoherently*] How dare you talk to me like the cracked Isaiah on the church window? As if you were somebody? For you weren't born to this. You weren't born to rap your own mother on the knuckles if she swipes a little bowl of salt someplace. Aren't you ashamed of yourself when you see how I tremble before you? You've made yourself their servant so no one will take their houses from them – houses they had stolen! Since when have houses belonged to the bedbugs? But you're on the watch, or they couldn't drag our men into their wars! You bribetaker! [AZDAK *half gets up, starts beaming. With his little hammer he half-heartedly knocks on the table as if to get silence. As* GRUSHA'S *scolding continues, he only beats time with his hammer.*] I've no respect for you. No more than for a thief or a bandit with a knife! You can do what you want. You can take the child away from me, a hundred against one, but I tell you one thing: only extortioners should be chosen for a profession like yours, and men who rape children! As punishment! Yes, let *them* sit in judgment on their fellow creatures. It is worse than to hang from the gallows.

AZDAK [*sitting down*]: Now it'll be thirty! And I won't go on squabbling with you – we're not in a tavern. What'd happen to my dignity as a judge? Anyway, I've lost interest in your case. Where's the couple who wanted a divorce? [*To* SHAUWA] Bring 'em in. This case is adjourned for fifteen minutes.

THE FIRST LAWYER [*to the* GOVERNOR'S WIFE]: Even without using the rest of the evidence, Madam, we have the verdict in the bag.

THE COOK [*to* GRUSHA]: You've gone and spoiled your chances with him. You won't get the child now.

THE GOVERNOR'S WIFE: Shalva, my smelling salts!

[*Enter a* VERY OLD COUPLE.]

AZDAK: I accept. [*The* OLD COUPLE *don't understand.*] I hear you want to be divorced. How long have you been together?

THE OLD WOMAN: Forty years, Your Honour.

AZDAK: And why do you want a divorce?

THE OLD MAN: We don't like each other, Your Honour.

AZDAK: Since when?

THE OLD WOMAN: Oh, from the very beginning, Your Honour.

AZDAK: I'll think about your request and render my verdict when I'm through with the other case. [SHAUWA *leads them back.*] I need the child. [*He beckons* GRUSHA *to him and bends not unkindly toward her.*] I've noticed you have a soft spot for justice. I don't believe he's your child, but if he *were* yours, woman, wouldn't you want him to be rich? You'd only have to say he wasn't yours, and he'd have a palace and many horses in his stables and many beggars on his doorstep and many soldiers in his service and many petitioners in his courtyard, wouldn't he? What do you say – don't you want him to be rich? [GRUSHA *is silent.*]

THE SINGER:

Hear now what the angry girl thought but did not say:

Had he golden shoes to wear
He'd be cruel as a bear.
Evil would his life disgrace.
He'd laugh in my face.

Carrying a heart of flint
Is too troublesome a stint.
Being powerful and bad
Is hard on a lad.

Then let hunger be his foe!
Hungry men and women, no.
Let him fear the darksome night
But not daylight!

AZDAK: I think I understand you, woman.

GRUSHA [*suddenly and loudly*]: I won't give him up. I've raised him, and he knows me.

[*Enter* SHAUWA *with the* CHILD.]

THE GOVERNOR'S WIFE: He's in rags!

GRUSHA: That's not true. But I wasn't given time to put his good shirt on.

THE GOVERNOR'S WIFE: He must have been in a pigsty.

GRUSHA [*furiously*]: I'm not a pig, but there are some who are! Where did you leave your baby?

THE GOVERNOR'S WIFE: I'll show you, you vulgar creature! [*She is about to throw herself on* GRUSHA, *but is restrained by* LAWYERS.] She's a criminal, she must be whipped. Immediately!

THE SECOND LAWYER [*holding his hand over her mouth*]: Natella Abashwili, you promised . . . Your Honour, the plaintiff's nerves . . .

AZDAK: Plaintiff and defendant! The Court has listened to your case, and has come to no decision as to who the real mother is. Therefore, I, the judge, am obliged to *choose* a mother for the child. I'll make a test. Shauwa, get a piece of chalk and draw a circle on the floor. [SHAUWA *does so*.] Now place the child in the centre. [SHAUWA *puts* MICHAEL, *who smiles at* GRUSHA, *in the centre of the circle*.] Stand near the circle, both of you. [*The* GOVERNOR'S WIFE *and* GRUSHA *step up to the circle*.] Now each of you take the child by one hand. [*They do so*.] The true mother is she who can pull the child out of the circle.

THE SECOND LAWYER [*quickly*]: High Court of Justice, I object! The fate of the great Abashwili estates, which are tied to the child, as the heir, should not be made dependent on such a doubtful duel. In addition, my client does not command the strength of this person, who is accustomed to physical work.

AZDAK: She looks pretty well fed to me. Pull! [*The*

GOVERNOR'S WIFE *pulls the* CHILD *out of the circle on her side;* GRUSHA *has let go and stands aghast.*] What's the matter with you? You didn't pull!

GRUSHA: I didn't hold on to him.

THE FIRST LAWYER [*congratulating the* GOVERNOR'S WIFE]: What did I say! The ties of blood!

GRUSHA [*running to* AZDAK]: Your Honour, I take back everything I said against you. I ask your forgiveness. But could I keep him till he can speak all the words? He knows a few.

AZDAK: Don't influence the Court. I bet you only know about twenty words yourself. All right, I'll make the test once more, just to be certain. [*The* TWO WOMEN *take up their positions again.*] Pull! [*Again* GRUSHA *lets go of the* CHILD.]

GRUSHA [*in despair*]: I brought him up! Shall I also tear him to bits? I can't!

AZDAK [*rising*]: And in this manner the Court has determined the true mother. [*To* GRUSHA] Take your child and be off. I advise you not to stay in the city with him. [*To the* GOVERNOR'S WIFE] And you disappear before I fine you for fraud. Your estates fall to the city. They'll be converted into a playground for the children. They need one, and I've decided it'll be called after me: Azdak's Garden. [*The* GOVERNOR'S WIFE *has fainted and is carried out by the* LAWYERS *and the* ADJUTANT. GRUSHA *stands motionless.* SHAUWA *leads the* CHILD *toward her.*] Now I'll take off this judge's gown – it's got too hot for me. I'm not cut out for a hero. In token of farewell I invite you all to a little dance in the meadow outside. Oh, I'd almost forgotten something in my excitement . . . to sign the divorce decree. [*Using the judge's chair as a table, he writes something on a piece of paper, and prepares to leave. Dance music has started.*]

SHAUWA [*having read what is on the paper*]: But that's not right. You've not divorced the old people. You've divorced Grusha!

AZDAK: Divorced the wrong couple? What a pity! And I

never retract! If I did, how could we keep order in the land? [*To the* OLD COUPLE] I'll invite you to my party instead. You don't mind dancing with each other, do you? [*To* GRUSHA *and* SIMON] I've got forty piastres coming from you.

SIMON [*pulling out his purse*]: Cheap at the price, Your Honour. And many thanks.

AZDAK [*pocketing the cash*]: I'll be needing this.

GRUSHA [*to* MICHAEL]: So we'd better leave the city tonight, Michael? [*To* SIMON] You like him?

SIMON: With my respects, I like him.

GRUSHA: Now I can tell you: I took him because on that Easter Sunday I got engaged to you. So he's a child of love. Michael, let's dance.

> [*She dances with* MICHAEL, SIMON *dances with the* COOK, *the* OLD COUPLE *with each other.* AZDAK *stands lost in thought. The dancers soon hide him from view. Occasionally he is seen, but less and less as* MORE COUPLES *join the dance.*]

THE SINGER:

And after that evening Azdak vanished and was never seen again.

The people of Grusinia did not forget him but long remembered

The period of his judging as a brief golden age.

Almost an age of justice.

> [ALL THE COUPLES *dance off.* AZDAK *has disappeared.*]

But you, you who have listened to the Story of the Chalk Circle,

Take note what men of old concluded:

That what there is shall go to those who are good for it,

Children to the motherly, that they prosper,

Carts to good drivers, that they be driven well,

The valley to the waterers, that it yield fruit.